Moral Warriors, Moral Wounds

Moral Warriors, Moral Wounds

THE MINISTRY OF THE CHRISTIAN ETHIC

≈

Wollom A. Jensen
James M. Childs, Jr.

CASCADE *Books* · Eugene, Oregon

MORAL WARRIORS, MORAL WOUNDS
The Ministry of the Christian Ethic

Cascade Books
An Imprint of Wipf and Stock Publishers
199 W. 8th Ave., Suite 3
Eugene, OR 97401

www.wipfandstock.com

Paperback ISBN 978-1-4982-2351-5
Hardcover ISBN 978-1-4982-2353-9
Ebook ISBN 978-1-4982-2352-2

Cataloging-in-Publication data:

Names: Jensen, Wollom A., and James M. Childs, Jr.

Title: Moral warriors, moral wounds : the ministry of the Christian ethic / Wollom A. Jensen and James M. Childs, Jr.

Description: Eugene, OR : Cascade Books, 2016 | Includes bibliographical references.

Identifiers: ISBN 978-1-4982-2351-5 (paperback) | ISBN 978-1-4982-2353-9 (hardcover) | ISBN 978-1-4982-2352-2 (ebook)

Subjects: 1. Armed Forces Chaplains. 2. Military Personnel psychology. 3. Just war tradition. I. Title.

Classification: U22.3 M490 2016 (print) | U22.3 (ebook)

Manufactured in the USA.

This book is dedicated to the women and men, veterans of combat, who were morally wounded because they were and remain moral warriors.

Contents

Contents

Chapter One

By Way of Introduction

THIS BOOK IS A thoroughly collaborative undertaking. At the same time, we each bring distinct experiences and qualifications to the task. Therefore, it seems good to us that we offer separate introductory comments in this opening chapter in order to give the reader a sense of what each of us brings to the conversation from our personal and professional formation.

Wollom A. "Wally" Jensen

St. Francis of Assisi was born into a culture of violence. Wars between city-states such as Assisi and Perugia were common and the tribal culture served to separate communities from one another are not unlike those which we experience in the twenty-first century. In 1202 at age twenty Francis became a soldier and went off to battle in a war between Assisi and Perugia. During this particular battle the Perugians defeated the Assisians. Francis was wounded during the battles and made a prisoner of war. For a long year Francis languished in a Perugian prison and was released only when his health began to deteriorate. While being held as a prisoner of war Francis began to reflect upon his life and his service as a soldier. As his health returned Francis continued to contemplate spiritual things more deeply. Eventually, Francis metamorphosized into the gentle monastic that many of us recognize today. Quite possibly Francis's health was complicated as a result of the moral injuries suffered by everyone who undergoes armed conflict as a warrior. In a very real and personal way for me, this part of the story of St. Francis is my story as well.

At age nineteen I entered into service in the United States Army as a volunteer draftee. I had spent my high school years involved in social activities such as band and athletics. I had been named "All Conference" in football, and was made the student director and first chair trumpet of my high school band. I had my own car, many friends, and enjoyed a relatively carefree life. I did well enough academically that I never worried about being accepted in a college and entertained dreams of going off to attend university at place like the United States Naval Academy, St. Olaf College, or the College of William and Mary. My mother and father had divorced when I was four years old, and I had been in the custody of my dad. My dad died of complications resulting from a stroke when I was sixteen and one of my dad's younger brothers became my guardian. Although no one in my family had graduated from college, it was assumed that I would attend a university and when I mentioned my interest in the three schools above I was told that I could go to any college I wanted to as long as it was in North Dakota. My options were obviously limited so I chose to enroll in the University of North Dakota at Grand Forks. Because of my immaturity, my anger about having been denied going to a school of my choice, and my carefree attitude, there was not much chance that I would be successful at the university level, and I wasn't. Social fraternity activities, the university marching band, and friends were high on my list of interests while study halls and class attendance were very low priorities. By the end of the second semester I had been invited by the dean of the College of Arts and Sciences to take a leave of absence from the university due to my exceptionally poor academic performance. In June, at the conclusion of my first academic year, I volunteered for the draft, and in August I was called up and found myself on my way to basic training at Ft. Lewis, Washington. Following graduation from Army Signal School at Ft. Gordon, Georgia and thirty days of leave over Christmas, by mid-February, 1968 I found myself in the Republic of South Vietnam assigned to the 125t Signal Battalion of the 25th Infantry Division. I arrived at Cu Chi, South Vietnam in the final throes of the 1968 Tet Offensive.

While I have no intention of drawing too close a parallel between my experience and that of St. Francis, I do have some understanding of his experience as a warrior and of being in combat. I know what it is to live with fear; to be appalled by the loss of human life; to be shamed by the experience of participating in war; and the feeling of having lost one's youth in ways that those who have not been to war will never be able to understand. I have experienced my own moral injury just as I'm convinced that St. Francis experienced moral injury. Not unlike Francis, I have sought relief from those injuries in the spiritual life and discipline of the church and in the call to ordained ministry in the church of my birth. Unlike Francis, however, I did not find my spiritual center of healing in a monastic community but rather in the community of warriors known as the United States Navy, where I spent nearly twenty-five years as a Sailor and chaplain to Sailors and Marines. It was in serving Sailors and Marines in the Sea Service that I came to feel that my combat experience was validated in that others shared my experience, gave it value, and affirmed it. I also came to realize that I had been injured morally, and that I had something to offer to other warriors by way of empathic pastoral care for them and their injuries as well. In a very real and personal way when I became a Navy chaplain it felt as though I had come home.

In this book my friend and colleague, Jim Childs, and I have attempted to articulate the ministry of military chaplaincy, the nature of moral wounds, and a way of reflection on the nature of war that is firmly grounded in the moral theology of the Christian community. It is our intention that this ethical reflection will be helpful to seminary professors who mentor chaplains or aspiring chaplains as they play key roles in the formation of those women and men for service in the ordained ministry of the church. We also intend that this book will serve as a pathway for those engaged in the work of chaplaincy within the military and in the veterans' communities where much of the healing work for veterans begins with the development of safe and sacred spaces in which to engage in the difficult and painful work of spiritual reflection. Finally, it is our hope that those warriors who are carrying a burden of guilt and shame will come to understand that not all wounds or injuries are necessarily fatal. There are at least three wounded warriors—St. Francis of Assisi; St. Ignatius of Loyola; and Wally Jensen—who through their own spiritual reflection and journeys, came to an understanding and awareness that God finds us where we are and reconciles us to himself through the bounty of his grace.

I hope that commanders who read this book will come to understand that they as well as those whom they command in combat are morally wounded. Those moral injuries are not always apparent. Frequently those moral injuries manifest themselves in medical problems that take on the characteristics of malingering. It is also not unusual that those moral injuries are acted out in disciplinary problems and inappropriate behaviors such as uncontrolled anger, family abuse, substance abuse and self-medication, and being absent without leave. Poor performance of duties may often be a sign of the presence of moral and spiritual injury.

Parish clergy and members of congregations as well who read this book may be helped to understand their moral and spiritual culpability in the burden of shame and guilt born by those who have gone to war on their behalf. "Thank you for your service," while well intentioned, does not carry the water unless it also carries the understanding of what that service entailed. It is important for both clergy and laity to understand that while there are indeed physical, psychological, and emotional injuries such as Traumatic Brain Injury, Post-Traumatic Stress, and others that require medical or psychological treatment regimens, there also injuries to the soul of warriors who have been involved in combat. These soul injuries are not medical or psychological in nature and therefore require a different modality of treatment. These soul injuries require what might be termed a faith-based modality. These injuries are theological and spiritual in nature and need to be treated with the tools of religion in order to bring about both spiritual healing and spiritual resilience. This reality obviously puts faith communities, congregations, clergy, and faithful laity on the front lines of spiritual triage and treatment. Unfortunately, most faith communities are ill equipped to respond to such injuries.

Francis of Assisi lived during an age in which the church was a major force in the lives and culture of the people. When Francis returned home to Assisi from Perugia following his captivity as a prisoner of war he entered a period of his life in which he engaged in deep spiritual reflection and self-assessment. Socrates asserted that an unexamined life is not worth living. He meant by this that a life whose values, morals, principles, underlying assumptions regarding happiness, sadness, suffering, and the meaning of existence which had not been thoroughly examined, critically evaluated, and internalized could never provide the basis for human flourishing— *eudaimonia*, or as it is described in the Gospel of St. John, "Abundant Life" (John 10:10). What emerged from Francis's examination of his life following and in light of his experience as a warrior and prisoner of war was a transformed man who found his previous life's values vapid and unable to give him either *eudaimonia* or abundant life. He gave away his possessions, entered into a deeply religious life marked by spiritual discipline, and began a new life quite different from his previous life of privilege and self-indulgence. In this transformation, Francis demonstrated what might today be called "resilience."

Resilience, though common in today's conversations about the physical, emotional, and psychological injuries suffered by those who have experienced combat, is not without its own controversy. The US Army has gone so far as to establish the Comprehensive Soldier and Family Fitness Program in 2009 at the direction of then Army Chief of Staff, General George Casey. Thinking of resilience as the ability of an object to return to its original shape following intense stress has been applied to individual warriors. Following the intense period of combat-induced stress the thinking is that if an individual can be given the requisite tools that individual has the capability to return to a state of normalcy. One of the major criticisms of resilience is the lack of a specific, objective definition. Without a commonly accepted definition of resilience research foci will be affected and the results will be untrustworthy. While the term *resiliency* can be helpful the considerable controversy surrounding it is causing some researchers to advocate for the abandonment of the term.

Nancy Sherman, writing in her book, *Afterwar: Healing the Moral Wounds of Our Soldiers*, says,

> Healing requires a complex understanding of one's war—how to make sense of its detritus and profound losses. Those losses can seem, on the one hand, all too futile in the face of war's often dubious and grand political goals, and on the other, thoroughly avoidable if only one's own conduct were just a bit more perfect. Repairing selves involves a kind of inner moral dialogue, a kind of call and response. Soldiers often feel need and hurt, and seek help that acknowledges that hurt and helps to redress it. Healing starts, then, from recognition and empathy; self-healing starts with self-empathy. All this takes time, loving support, and intellectual honesty. For many in the military, it is still all too easy to soft-peddle the realities of mental and moral injury, and to believe that with just a little bit more positive thinking and stoic sucking it up, they can get the mission done. But healing after moral trauma is not that kind of mission. Thriving after war requires a different kind of resilience.[1]

Moral wounds require moral healing. Military chaplains represent the first responders, those called to provide triage to the badly wounded, bringing the tools, training, and skills to help stop the spiritual hemorrhaging of

1. Sherman, *Afterwar*, 80–81.

those who have been morally though not necessarily mortally wounded in combat. This book is dedicated to those moral first responders and intended to introduce all others to an awareness and understanding of the nature of the ministry of military chaplains.

James M. "Jim" Childs, Jr.

My colleague in this endeavor, Wally Jensen, and I met by chance at a conference of ethicists dealing with issues of just war and related concerns; he was one of the speakers. We ended up in the same small group and "connected." Our conversation led to an agreement to work on this resource in military ethics. Happily, this agreement to collaborate also led to our friendship, which has progressed along with the work on this book.

Wally says a few things about his youth. Here we share some common ground. I was all-conference in football and went on to play football on scholarship for a time at Brown University in the late fifties. However, being musically disadvantaged, I never played the trumpet as he did. I tried for a bit in grammar school but my parents decided the $15 fee was better spent on a new muffler for the old Ford! In college I also found myself drifting from any clear sense of values. Though making my grades, I was far more immersed in fraternity parties and football. Wally's path as he describes it was to military service, eventually combat experience in Vietnam, and later to ministry and Naval chaplaincy. My path of self-rediscovery was to the ministry. I served as a white pastor in an African American church in the South during the middle of the turbulent sixties and eventually ended up teaching theology and ethics in college, university, and seminary for the past forty-six years.

Along the way I have had more than my share of personal experience of conflict and loss due to being deeply involved in church-related controversies. I mention this not to suggest for a minute that the experience and the pain of such conflicts compare to those of warriors in harm's way. Nonetheless, these ecclesial conflicts between sisters and brothers in the same faith community over matters of theology and ethics, often involving serious matters of social justice, can become deeply divisive and even vicious; they have the capacity to traumatize participants both emotionally and spiritually and in some cases lead to a sense of dislocation and loss of faith and ministry. What this kind of experience adds to my contribution to our enterprise is a deepened sense of realism about the hurtful capacities of human beings everywhere and, I sincerely hope, a greater sensitivity to all wounded spirits. That said, I would not have undertaken this journey of a Christian perspective on military ethics without the partnership of Wally Jensen, who brings a depth of military experience as both soldier and chaplain that lends credibility to our efforts.

Over the years I have taught Christian ethics in terms of its theological foundations and various methodological expressions, including the development of my own basic approach, which is spelled out in my book, *Ethics in the Community of Promise*,[2] and which is referenced at a number of points in this book. I have taught moral philosophy in university and business ethics at the MBA level. I have worked on the correlation of these disciplines and the discipline of Christian ethics. I have taught and written about various topics of applied ethics. However, except for a bit of work on just war theory, one area of applied ethics I have not dealt with heretofore is military ethics. As a result, this has been a challenging learning experience and a rewarding one as well.

Each of the fields of applied ethics has its own particular issues. The task for the ethicist is to apply what he or she regards as universally valid principles and values to the specific issues of a given area of concern, which has its own terminology, array of salient facts, and inherent logic. For the Christian ethicist this also means engaging the perspectives of moral philosophers who are also working at the same task. The field of biomedical ethics, for example, involves many different areas of ethical engagement, including everything from end-of-life decisions to fetal stem cell research to professional conduct to experimental protocols and more. In any of these areas the ethicist needs to be acquainted with the relevant scientific data, the legal dimensions, the ethos of the profession, and, in many cases, revealing case material, not to mention the testimony of the experience of all parties involved. With all of the many considerations in play the process of ethical reasoning can become complex and at times uncertain and ambiguous. Military ethics poses the same demands for the consideration of relevant facts and experiences. Certainly the ethos and traditions of the services are a major factor. Legal realities are as prominent here as in the fields of biomedical ethics, as are considerations of the ethics of professional conduct. One can find parallels in other fields of applied ethics. Organizational ethics and ethical leadership principles can resonate with the organizational realities and the leadership demands of the military.

---

2. Childs, *Ethics in the Community of Promise*.

Yet, when all is said and done, there are ways in which military ethics might be judged, at least at first blush, as distinct from these other fields of applied ethics. Biomedical ethics is operating in a field of endeavor that seeks to prevent illness, heal, relieve pain, and enhance and preserve life (notwithstanding controversy over matters such as assisted dying and fetal stem cell research); this is its overarching metanarrative. The common good is also the focus of the ethics of economic justice and ecojustice. Certainly, the overarching purpose of the military is to insure and maintain peace and therefore serve the preservation of life and the common good. That should never be forgotten. Certainly, there are tough decisions in other fields where the lesser of evils may, after all considerations, be the only choice. However, for the military the inescapable reality of choosing the lesser evil is codified in just war theory, which provides the governing framework for doing military ethics. For its warriors "the lesser evil" is lived out in the chaos and terrors of battle.

Plotting how ethics apply in other fields, then, has many similarities to the challenges of doing military ethics. Yet the practitioners in those other endeavors are not trained killers or the leaders or trainers or supporters of trained killers. Does this purpose of killing the enemy, albeit for the sake of a just cause and as a last resort, make the task of military ethics distinct from all other expressions of applied ethics? I suspect that the answer is "yes and no." The task of military ethics is not distinct in that it participates in the brokenness and ambiguity that is common to the experience of all human-kind and that is the enduring reality within which all ethical reasoning and moral striving must operate and often languish. Crafting an ethic for the military involves using the same principles, values, and reasoning found in all fields of ethics. And all applied ethics needs to be sensitive to the human realities involved. Ethics cannot be merely an exercise in abstract formulas. However, doing military ethics means applying those principles and values common to all ethics to situations in which life is at risk and the horrors of war can be its living context. It is an ethic for people called upon to kill other human beings at peril of their own souls. Some may relish that role; most do not. This makes the task distinct.

Beside the constant danger to life and limb, the moral and spiritual burden warriors bear for their service of possible and actual killing deserves the utmost care and consideration. The ethics of military service must be surrounded by compassion and care. It needs to be an ethics that is more than ethics but also a vision of survival for one's humanity and spiritual well-being in a radically ambiguous moral context of warfare. We think that Christian ethics can speak to that need. The Christian ethic operates in the context of faith in divine grace and presence despite the ambiguities and uncertainties of moral striving in a world broken by sin and evil.

Dietrich Bonhoeffer quotes Luther, "*Pecca fortiter, sed fortius fide at gaude in Christo.*" "Sin boldly, but believe and rejoice in Christ even more boldly." Bonhoeffer explains that Luther did not mean to suggest that we can feel free to sin since we know that God will forgive us. Rather, it was intended as encouragement for those who are paralyzed by the realization that they cannot live free from sin in this world no matter how hard they try. The world of our making is fraught with uncertainties, inescapably tragic choices, and ambiguity. These fragile spirits are encouraged by Luther to enter into life and its difficult challenges with the robust faith that God is with them even when their best efforts fall short.[3] I tell my students in ethics classes that as Christians we do not pursue the moral life of neighbor love with the presumption of *certitude*, the conviction that we can always know and do precisely what is the clear will of God even under the most complex circumstances. Such an expectation is doomed to either self-righteous self-deception or radical disappointment and even despair. Rather, we live by *assurance* of God's gracious presence as we seek to do the will of God in a radically imperfect world. Nowhere does this truth of faith apply more readily than in the living out the Christian ethic in the context of military service. It is in this spirit that we have approached the issues of military ethics.

We have tried to correlate principles and values of the Christian ethic of love with the stated values and virtues of the services. We have tried to show that an ethic of Christian love can speak meaningfully even in the situation of war. How can one speak of *agape* love in such a context? We think one can. And we think that the Christian ethic, with its stark realism and assurance of divine grace can do more than give directions about right and wrong; it can speak to the spiritual health of those caught in some of life's worst heart-rending situations.

Wally has already spoken of the audiences we hope to reach. While the chaplains feature prominently among those to whom we speak, we hope that they and others can be a link to the ministry of Christian faith communities for the support of those who serve and for engagement in seeking the well-being of the wounded. The overwhelming majority of people in

3. Bonhoeffer, *Discipleship*, 51–52.

9

our nation are not in the military and never will be but, in a real sense, we all are for they are part of us and serve for us. The more all of us know about the moral realities of military existence, the more compassionate and intelligent we will be as supporters of our service people and as voices in the policies of our government. Indeed, in the academic study of Christian ethics its application in military ethics should be the interest of all teachers and students of Christian ethics, not just those in the military or preparing for military chaplaincy; the questions of military ethics can in certain cases provide a critical test for the viability of one's ethical vision and method. At least, I have found it so.

PART I

The Chaplain and the Challenges of Military Culture

Chapter Two

The Vocation of the Chaplain

BEFORE WE CAN ENTER into the discussion of military ethics, Christian ethics, and the role of the chaplain, which is a main focus of this book, it is necessary to be clear about the vocation of military chaplaincy. As we shall see presently, military chaplains share much the same vocational formation and many of the same vocational duties as the other clergy of their faith communities. However, it is the very fact that military chaplains do share in the vocational identity of other clergy that serves to highlight the ways in which their calling differs. In a word, their commitment in military service involves requirements that draw on the theological and ecclesial sources shared with other clergy but, at the same time, may stand in real tension with those sources. Consequently, accepting the calling to military chaplaincy itself involves profound ethical questions of integrity.

Setting the Stage

Chaplains have served in the military of the United States beginning with the Continental Army during the Revolutionary War. The Continental Congress authorized the Army to hire its first military chaplain in 1791.[1] Military chaplaincy is rooted within the First Amendment of the US Constitution regarding religious freedom, free speech and freedom of the press, the right of peaceful assembly, and the right to petition the government for the redress of grievances.

---

1. Lasson, "Religious Liberty in the Military."

> Congress shall make no law respecting an establishment of religion, or prohibiting the free exercise thereof; or abridging the freedom of speech, or of the press; or the right of the people peaceably to assemble, and to petition the Government for a redress of grievances.

The heart of religious liberty is, of course, located in the first phrase of the amendment and consists of two clauses. These two clauses are often referred to as the Establishment Clause and the Free Exercise Clause. There exists within these two clauses a built-in tension that, when in balance, protects the people from a governmental establishment of any religion, and an individual's right to freely practice his or her personal religious beliefs. While the legal discussions and court decisions regarding the jurisprudence related to these two clauses are complex, suffice it to say that because of the requirements related to military service members are often required to be separated from their religious communities for extended periods of time. Therefore religious services offered by military chaplains and which are not forced upon members of the military have been deemed to be constitutional. It is instructive to note that the basis for military chaplains is not related to the religious rights of the chaplain, but rather the basis for military chaplaincy is rooted in the constitutional guarantees and protections of individual service members. In order to comply with the constitutional requirements as stated within the First Amendment the Department of Defense provides oversight and guidance through implementation of directives and instructions addressing the religious practices within the armed services. It is helpful to understand the differences between directives and instructions.

- A DOD Directive is the highest authority within the Department of Defense. As such, a Department of Defense Directive establishes policy, delegates authority, and assigns responsibility related to a particular issue within the Department of Defense.

- A Department of Defense Instruction implements the policy established within a Department of Defense Directive.

Military chaplains wear at least two professional "hats" or carry two separate controlling interests. First, a military chaplain is a commissioned officer appointed by the president of the United States to the particular service branch in a specified grade, i.e., rank. As such, the chaplain, as all commissioned officers, swears an oath of allegiance to support and defend the

Constitution of the United States against all enemies, foreign and domestic. Additionally, the military chaplain must, as all commissioned officers must, meet all of the requirements, including education, experience, the ability to successfully obtain the necessary security clearances, and physical standards as established by the Department of Defense and specific service branch.

Second, a military chaplain must meet all of the requirements of a specific faith community necessary to carry out the unique religious requirements as established by that faith community. These requirements include education, professional training and experience, ministry competence, and spiritual formation required of all professional representatives of the chaplains faith community. Normally these professional ministerial requirements lead to ordination or designation as a professional member of the clergy of the faith community. Once these requirements have been met, the chaplain's faith community, that has been recognized by the Department of Defense under the auspices of the Armed Forces Chaplain's Board—a group consisting of the Chiefs of Chaplains of the Army, Navy, and Air Force—provides official ecclesiastical endorsement to the Chief of Chaplains of the specific branch of service into which the chaplain will be commissioned. The ecclesiastical endorsement comes in the form of a Department of Defense (DD) form 2088 and certifies that the chaplain has met all of the requirements necessary to represent the specific faith community as a military chaplain.

From the very start of a military chaplain's service, the chaplain finds him or herself in something of an ethical bind. The chaplain who dons the uniform of a military chaplain is a commissioned officer with all of the rights and responsibilities attending to that office. The chaplain is also an ecclesiastically endorsed representative of the faith community that has provided the certification of chaplain's good standing as a representative of that community. Frequently the chaplain must negotiate the ethical tensions which exist between the needs of the military and the teaching tenets of the endorsing ecclesiastical community. For military chaplains, life is lived in the interstices of the military service and the civilian religious community.

The beginning point for any chaplaincy is located in a specific faith community's unique process for preparing an individual to serve as an ordained clergyperson within it. This process belongs solely to the individual faith community and reflects its theology and traditions. No two faith communities are exactly alike and, in fact, there are slight differences reflected even within individual communities depending upon the number of seminaries or divinity schools, the number of judicatories existent within the faith communities, and the internal homogeneity or diversity of the faith communities. The predictable outcome of this reality is that clergy are not prepared in exactly the same way nor do they have exactly the same qualifications. There is no cookie cutter mold to the preparation of clergy.

Among the most important personal and professional clergy attributes identified by various faith communities are well-formed leaders who possess stable character and mature faith. Certainly faith communities rightfully expect that their religious leaders will be holy men and women who are equipped to rise up to the challenge of living personally and professionally a life of sanctity. In order to meet this challenge the clergy must be equipped with the disciplines that yield lifelong growth in their faith and practice. When referring specifically to Christian clergy one might borrow from the Eastern Orthodox who use the term *theosis* to describe the lifelong transformational process of becoming ever more godlike until we begin to participate in the divine nature, or as St. Paul describes it, we are being changed into the likeness of Christ from one degree of glory to another (2 Cor 3:18).

Once commissioned a military chaplain undergoes the basic military training for a chaplain officer. The military school for the Military Chaplains is located at the Armed Forces Chaplaincy Center in at Fort Jackson, South Carolina. The Armed Forces Chaplaincy Center (AFCC) hosts the United States Army Chaplaincy Center and School; the United States Naval Chaplaincy School and Center; and the United States Air Force Corps College. The AFCC provides the basic military knowledge for newly commissioned Chaplain Corps Officers to be able to effectively function at their first active duty stations. In addition to customs and traditions of each individual service, the students at AFCC learn military bearing, discipline, and gain a basic knowledge of field ministry skills. These chaplain students also learn the reality of working not only in a joint service environment but in an intensely pluralistic environment that daily challenges their identity and formation as clergy representatives of their individual faith communities and ecclesiastical endorsing bodies. These are but the first of many ethical and moral challenges that chaplain corps officers will face throughout their military service.

The initial and in many ways one of the most significant of the ethical/moral challenges these new chaplain corps officers will face will greet them as they begin their Chaplain Corps Basic Course, namely, the issue of pluralism. Bishop James Magness, a retired Navy chaplain and current Episcopal Bishop for Armed Forces and Federal Ministries, is fond of describing military chaplaincy as being beyond ecumenism and fully immersed not only into pluralism, but pluralism on steroids. Military chaplaincy is a world of theological and interfaith diversity with which most clergy have only passing experience. Practicing the professional craft of ministry within the context of an intensely pluralistic environment poses challenges that simply do not exist for those living out their professional vocations within the civilian and particularly the congregational setting. What's the difference?

Congregational ministry is uniquely denominational. Parish clergy are called to serve a specific faith community and typically are trained and formed within the tradition of that community. Although the process of formation is unique to each faith tradition, clergy called to serve within the denomination all experience a similar and recognizable process of formation within the particular community. The differences in professional formation within the Christian tradition are often profound. Roman Catholic, Eastern Orthodox, and most mainline Protestant denominations require a bachelor's degree followed by a Master of Divinity degree earned at one of the denomination's theological seminaries or at an accredited and recognized divinity school. Following or as part of the education process the individual preparing for ordained ministry is often required to serve an internship or a period of service as a transitional deacon prior to ordination as a professional minister. This is often not the case for those Christians coming out of a Pentecostal background. While not the standard neither is it unusual for a Pentecostal minister to be ordained and called to serve a large congregation with a significant budget after having attended an unaccredited bible college and without having earned a Master of Divinity but having been duly recognized as one who has been called and anointed for ministry by the Holy Spirit. While all of the processes for preparation and training of ordained clergy work for their individual denominations, they do not all work equally well when it comes to serving in a broadly pluralistic institutional ministry such as that found within the military services.

During the period of time from the mid-1990s until the present there have been numerous lawsuits initiated alleging widespread discrimination against chaplains who have received ecclesiastical endorsement from evangelical bodies. Most of the litigation asserts that mainline denominations have assumed positions of power and influence that has resulted in prefer-ential treatment with regard to desirable assignments and promotion op-portunities. These lawsuits are rooted in the perception, rightly or wrongly, that certain groups have been given preferential treatment which has re-sulted in a disproportionate number of mainline chaplains in senior ranks and assignments to positions widely believed to be career enhancing. One of the many legal cases resulting from the notion that evangelical Chris-tian chaplains were discriminated against was *Larson v. US Navy*, a federal district course case decided in 2007 (486 F. Supp.2nd 11[D.D.C. 2007]). The Larson case was brought by three nonliturgical Protestant chaplains who challenged the Navy's practice of hiring according to a "thirds" policy. Although it was never clearly established that such a policy was ever in place, the litigants argued that the Navy chaplain corps had been divided into thirds (Roman Catholic, liturgical Protestant, and nonliturgical Chris-tian and Special Worship), which they contended was inadequate to meet the constitutional requirement guaranteeing the free exercise of service members. The terms liturgical Protestant and nonliturgical Christian were long used to describe those groups who baptized infants and those who do not baptize infants. Today these two groups are loosely defined as mainline Protestants and evangelicals. The Special Worship category includes Or-thodox Christians, Jews, Muslims, and all others.

The court declared the question regarding the so-called thirds policy moot because the policy was not in place at the time of the lawsuit. What the *Larson* case did establish, however, is that the Navy has neither the re-sources nor the requirement to meet the specific religious needs of each service member. However, the constitutional principle that accommoda-tions are permissible if they broadly facilitate opportunities to alleviate burdens imposed upon individual religious exercise was upheld.[2] Fol-lowing the *Larson* decision the Department of Defense established policy published in DOD Directive 1304.19 that the chaplaincies of each military department exist for three purposes: (1) to "advise and assist commanders in the discharge of their responsibilities to provide for the free exercise of religion in the context of military service as guaranteed by the Constitu-tion"; (2) to "assist commanders in managing Religious Affairs"; and (3) to "serve as the principal advisors to commanders for all issues regarding the impact of religion on military operations."[3] Perhaps most importantly for

2. Mason and Brougher, *Military Personnel and Freedom of Religious Expression*, 15.
3. Ibid.

the consideration of the professional requirements of clergy serving within the Department of Defense arising out of the *Larson* case is that clergy who are going to be considered for an appointment as a chaplain in one of the military departments must "provide an endorsement from a qualified religious organization verifying, among many things, that the individual is willing to function in a pluralistic environment . . . and is willing to support directly and indirectly the free exercise of religion by all members of the Military Services, their family members, and other persons authorized to be served by the military chaplaincies. Further, applicants for appointment as chaplains must affirm that they will abide by applicable laws, and all applicable regulations, directives, and instructions of the Department of Defense, and of the military Departments that grades the appointment.[4]

While certain professional requirements have been established they are necessarily broad. The First Amendment precludes the government from establishing too specific requirements and requires that each qualified religious organization must still establish its own unique professional requirements for applicants requesting ecclesiastical endorsement. As is often the case with legal decisions there are unintended consequences that result. There is no indication that litigation resulting from real or perceived religious discrimination is diminishing. It is also a reality that the tensions between religious organizations has not diminished and when para-church organizations such as CRU (formally Campus Crusade for Christ), or the Navigators are added to the pluralistic environment, the tensions have actually increased, making for an even more challenging pluralistic context in which clergy serving within the Department of Defense are called to serve.

The differences in preparation and theological tradition coupled with the demands of pluralism suggest the real need for a faith-based approach to military ethics that is shareable among chaplains of diverse backgrounds.[5] That is our goal. Such a resource would find its place in the exercise of assistance to commanders mandated in DOD Directive 1304.19

---

4. Ibid., 15–16.

5. Peter French, a philosophy professor, was engaged by the Navy during the Iraq conflict to provide ethics training for chaplains. Commenting on the wide range of academic preparation from rigorous theological schools to Bible colleges and conservative seminaries with narrow curricula, French observed, "In my early years as a college philosophy professor, I taught large undergraduate courses in which the academic abilities of students varied dramatically, but I could not recall teaching such a radically diverse group in terms of academic preparation as those chaplains . . . ." French, *War and Moral Dissonance*, 7.

cited above. For example, it fits in purpose with Department of the Army (Army Regulation 165–1): "Army Chaplain Corps Activities," the section on Moral Leadership Training indicates that this is the commander's religious program for which the chaplain is the staff officer responsible for conducting the program, etc. "The commander will approve all teaching subjects." And in addition to recommended training materials, "Preparation and use of original materials by individual Chaplains, in coordination with local commanders and their staff officers is encouraged."

Though we will be writing from our perspective as Christians we do not do so from a doctrinaire stance. Our hope is that, therefore, chaplains of other faiths will be able to benefit when looking at the text through the lens of their own faith and experience.

Vocational Integrity

The Ministry and the Military Chaplaincy: Common Features and Special Challenges

The first step toward our goal is to give further consideration to the vocation of the military chaplaincy and its inherent ethical challenge to honor commitments to God and country with integrity. We begin with a few observations about the call military chaplains share with other ministers.

Theologies of ministry differ as well as patterns of ecclesial endorsement. But all ecclesial endorsements, however defined and implemented, carry with them a clear sense of "call." This call, this sense of a real vocation, is presumed to be rooted in the candidate's spiritual discernment, nurtured through education and formation, and affirmed by the person's faith community. An entailment of that call, once conferred and accepted, is loyalty to the theological tradition of the church body that has entrusted the person with its ministry. Chaplains share this commitment with all other clergy. Chaplains also share the same duties and practices of ministry with other clergy as well. These include continuance in the study of sacred texts, faithfulness in prayer, theologically informed preaching, administration of the sacraments where applicable, pastoral care and counseling, and teaching. Issues of life and death are common to all clergy just as they may dominate the work of the hospital or hospice chaplain or share in some of the heartbreak particular to ministry in hospitals for children. For military chaplains in combat matters of life, death, and injury can certainly have their own particular traumatic characteristics, given the horrors of war. Nonetheless, ministry to the dying, the sick, or injured and comfort for those who grieve is a function shared with the ministry in general.

Other authorized ministries, though, share a common vocation and face different responsibilities, depending on their circumstances and the demands of their specific call. Thus, parish pastors, professional counselors, hospital, nursing home or hospice chaplains, military chaplains, prison chaplains, seminary professors, etc., claim the same vocational status as clergy but must interpret the theological substance of that vocation in terms appropriate to their location in the work of the ministry.

Again, all in authorized ministries, it may be presumed, share the sense of call and the theological loyalties that entails, whether serving in a congregation or in various other settings. The special challenges military chaplains face in relation to that call may not be unique but they seem to us to be more pronounced than those in other special ministries. These challenges or potential sources of tension have already been named: the commitment to serve in pluralistic settings and the difficulties that can arise in reconciling apparently conflicting demands of the dual commitment to God (one's call) and country. The first of these may at times be a factor in the second. As stated at the outset, these realities involve military chaplains ethically in a number of ways that can be gathered up under the heading of "integrity."

An Honest Theology for a Pluralistic Context

While increasing numbers of clergy and their church bodies are open to ecumenical cooperation and even interfaith conversation, their call usually does not entail an intentional ecumenical theology or even a clear understanding of other faiths, as desirable as these may be. Military chaplains do not have this option; they need to have a clear understanding of how their own theological commitments relate to those of other traditions with whom they will be intimately involved under often stressful circumstances.

Theologian Ted Peters has identified three different approaches that theologians and church bodies have taken to interacting with other faiths. The first of these is called "Confessional Universalism." Those who take this approach clearly affirm the authentic claims of their faith but remain open to the insights of others. This requires readiness for dialogue. Dialogue has its own ethical character because it entails respect for one's partner in the dialogue and an honest exchange of views. One must state one's own position truthfully and be open sympathetically to that which the person from the other tradition is advancing. Dialogue is not debate with winners and losers; it is, we would say, a path of discovery and mutual trust. One must care about the other and genuinely seek points of unity, with a desire to see one's dialogue partner edified by what one shares rather than judged by it. And, Peters emphasizes, it takes time and stamina to continue working at it and seeking greater depth and thoroughness through the process.[6] The second outlook is labeled "Confessional Exclusivism." As the label suggests, this position brooks no alternative to its own faith tradition. There is no purpose in dialogue since holders of this view believe their knowledge is complete and absolute.[7] Some who adhere to this conviction may believe that there is no salvation outside their faith.

Finally, we have what Peters calls "Supraconfessional Universalism." Simply stated, adherents of this view believe all religions point to the same transcendent reality and all have a partial share of its revelation. Consequently, normative claims made by various religious traditions are merely a product of human narrow-mindedness. There is little to be expected from dialogue as previously described since there can be no authentically normative claims to be shared and explored for further insight.[8] One might suppose that interesting conversation might be the most likely outcome of interaction.

While Peters is speaking about interfaith relationships, it is not difficult to see corollaries to these categories in attitudes among different traditions within the same faith community. Certainly within faith communities that display different traditions and theological emphases there are exclusivists on behalf of one particular expression of the faith who find it hard to reconcile theologically with those outside their dogmatic orbit. Confessional exclusivists will find it hard to operate in a pluralistic context. An honest appraisal of whether one belongs in that category must precede commitment to military chaplaincy. If that outlook fits, how will one answer the call to *minister* in a pluralist context, rather than offer half-hearted service or to see those of other faiths simply as one's mission field?

The missional fervor often characteristic of exclusivism is illustrated by the following account. From 2003–2005 the Rev. Kristen J. Leslie, a

---

6. Peters, *God—The World's Future*, 353–54.

7. Ibid., 354.

8. Ibid., 361–62.

professor of pastoral care at the Yale University Divinity School, was engaged as a consultant to the chaplains at the United States Air Force Academy. The report of her work there led to her testimony before the House Armed Services Committee in June of 2005 as part of the congressional investigation of allegations of religious intolerance and Christian proselytizing at the Academy. Her discoveries were stunning. "The majority of the Christian chaplains understood their pastoral role to be that of Christian evangelist."[9] One of the chaplains returning from deployment in Iraq told of conducting baptisms of service members in Saddam's pool. "The triumph of Christianity over Islam was lost on no one."[10]

> During a general Protestant worship service, a chaplain admonished 600 cadets in attendance to return to their tents and proselytize their bunkmates, reminding them that those who were not "born again will burn in the fires of hell." In the civilian world such an admonition from the pulpit would be seen as appropriately located. In this military environment, however, chaplains are also officers who have the power to give and receive orders. In such a system, a call to evangelize can be understood as a direct order from a superior officer.[11]

There is by contrast a strong historical tradition in the military chaplaincy that has been described as "cooperative pluralism," in which chaplains understand themselves to be ". . . pastor to some, chaplain to all. That is, they are pastors or religious professionals using their liturgical, sacramental, and historical authority . . . to serve the dietary, communal and spiritual needs of their particular faith group. And they are chaplains to any member of the community, regardless of religious confession, who wants the spiritual and institutional support offered by a religious professional."[12]

The description of "cooperative pluralism" just given is a practice that fits nicely with the confessional universalist perspective, which we commend. Confessional universalism seems to us to preserve the integrity of one's theological tradition—the theological teaching one swore to uphold at ordination or its equivalent—while yet displaying openness to the faith and needs of others. Its dialogical orientation embodies the fundamental ethical principle of respect for persons, which is another way of saying

9. Leslie, "Pastoral Care in a New Public, 87.

10. Ibid.

11. Ibid., 87–88.

12. Ibid., 92.

respect for the autonomy of others. Respect for autonomy also expresses justice as fairness. Both of these are basic ethical norms that will be with us throughout this discussion. They fit with the character of servant leadership that will be developed in the next chapter. In addition, it is also an ethical requirement of leadership in general and military chaplaincy in particular to commit to competency. In the context of pluralism, competency involves gaining knowledge of the various religious traditions not only through dialogue but also through study.

There are a number of informative sources for such study. A good introductory text is Michael D. Coogan's *The Illustrated Guide to World Religions* (New York: Oxford, 2003). The BBC has an introductory internet resource on world religions at http://bbc.co.uk/religio/religions. Of particular interest is the extensive information available on the website of the Harvard Pluralism project, http://pluralism.org. The goals stated on the site for this project undertaken in the face of our increasingly pluralistic society are as follows:

1. To document and better understand the changing contours of American religious demography, focusing especially on those cities and towns where the new plurality has been most evident and discerning the ways in which this plurality is both visible and invisible in American public life.

2. To study the religious communities themselves—their temples, mosques, gurudwaras, and retreat centers, their informal networks and emerging institutions, their forms of adaptation and religious education in the American context, their encounter with the other religious traditions of our common society, and their encounter with civic institutions.

3. To explore the ramifications and implications of America's new plurality through case studies of particular cities and towns, looking at the response of Christian and Jewish communities to their new neighbors; the development of interfaith councils and networks; the new theological and pastoral questions that emerge from the pluralistic context; and the recasting of traditional church-state issues in a wider context.

4. To discern, in light of this work, the emerging meanings of religious "pluralism," both for religious communities and for public institutions, and to consider the real challenges and opportunities of a public

commitment to pluralism in the light of the new religious contours of America.

The supraconfessional universalist will obviously be at home in any pluralistic setting. However, the question arises as to whether or not one can effectively represent the strong themes of a given tradition that its members long for in times of spiritual or physical need. Still it is certainly possible that chaplains who hold this position can accommodate to the convictions of those served for the sake of providing ministry. The faith-based ethic that will unfold as we proceed, though cognizant of life's ambiguities and far from legalistic in its reasoning, is still grounded in firmly held distinctive theological convictions.

God and Country

The tension a person of faith may experience between service to the faith, to God, and service in the military as a representative of that faith is one that needs to be faced at the point of deciding whether or not to enter the chaplaincy. Service in the military is sworn service to the state and thereby to the common good that the military exists to protect and preserve. Chaplains share in this service. Even though they are not combatants, they also share in the reality that military service can involve armed combat and killing with rigorous training for that possibility. In today's voluntary military services each prospective service member will have to discern whether or not their conscience will allow participation in violence before making a commitment. Chaplains must also be faithful to the dictates of their conscience. Moreover, they are also authorized representatives of their faith tradition. Therefore, if they are able and willing in good conscience to enter the military chaplaincy, it is incumbent upon them to have a clearly developed theological rationale for people of their faith being involved in war. Such a rationale is needed 1) to undergird their own conscientious decision; 2) to demonstrate faithfulness to their theological tradition; and 3) as a resource for ministry to service members who are struggling with issues of war and conscience. Historically, persons of faith in the military and in the chaplaincy have turned to just war theory for help toward this end.

Just war theory has played a crucial role in providing nations and their military services with a rationale for engaging in war. Just war thinking in the Christian tradition goes back at least as far as Ambrose of Milan in the fourth century and has been prominently associated with such towering figures as Augustine, Thomas Aquinas, and Martin Luther. Although just war theory is continually being interpreted and reevaluated in light of contemporary conditions, it remains the key referent in the development of military ethics. Because of this foundational role and the important discussion of how it can function in today's world, we will be giving just war theory further consideration in chapter 9. For the present it is sufficient to recall the basic criteria. This is one commonplace account. Other accounts may show slight variations in wording and listing but not really in substance.[13]

- *War must be declared by a legitimate authority:* This means there should be a public declaration. It precludes sneak attacks and represents the legal exercise of authority on the part of the government. In these days when war is being engaged against insurgents or terrorists attacking a nation in need of outside military help, the agreement of a coalition of concerned nations or organizations like NATO and the UN becomes an important factor in legitimating international intervention and in applying the other criteria.[14]

- *War must be fought only for a just cause:* This may include defense against unprovoked aggression, defense of one's allies, deterrence of a threat to peace, or humanitarian assistance to those under oppression.

- *War must be fought with the right intention:* The decision to go to war must be motivated by a desire for peace and the common good and not out of revenge, ethnic hatred, the will to power, or material or territorial gain.

- *War must be a last resort:* All means to avoid war—such as diplomatic measures, economic sanctions, or some form of international inspection or ongoing scrutiny—should be exhausted.

13. See Childs, *Ethics in the Community of Promise,* 185–86. See also the listing under "War" in the *Stanford Encyclopedia of Philosophy.*

14 "The Charter of the United Nations provides the modern treaty framework for *jus ad bellum.* Under the charter of the United Nations, the U.N. Security Council has primary responsibility for the maintenance of international peace and security The U.N. Security Council may determine the existence of any threat to the peace, breach of the peace, or act of aggression, and may decide what measures shall be taken under the Charter to maintain or restore international peace and security. For example, the U.N. Security Council may recognize that a State is acting lawfully in self-defense or another state is the aggressor in an armed conflict. In addition, the U.N. Security Council may authorize the use of military force." *Department of Defense Law of War Manual,* 1.11.2.

- *The values gained by the war effort should be proportionately greater than the evils of war itself:* This precludes war efforts that are futile and requires that the decision to go to war calculates in advance the probability of a proportionally greater good resulting.

These criteria provide guidance as to whether or not it is just to go to war, *jus ad bellum.* The following two criteria speak to how war should be waged if it is considered just, *jus in bello.*

- *War must be waged in respect for the lives of noncombatants:* Notwithstanding the fact that modern warfare has exacted huge civilian casualties, the principle of attacking only those who are combatants remains.[15]

- *The means used must be proportionate to the ends.* This criterion precludes "overkill," using more force and doing more damage than is needed to achieve the mission.

To these two traditional criteria for *jus in bello,* others would add:

- *Benevolent treatment of prisoners:* As provided by the Geneva Conventions, prisoners, no longer being combatants, should be kept from battle zones, and should not be subjected to death, torture, starvation, rape, medical experimentation, etc.

- *No Means Mala in Se:* Soldiers may not use weapons or methods that are inherently evil. These include mass rape campaigns, genocide or ethnic cleansing, using poison or treachery (like disguising soldiers to look like Red Cross personnel), and using weapons whose effects cannot be controlled such as biological or other chemical weapons.

The *Department of Defense Law of War Manual* speaks to these latter two principles of *jus in bello* in terms of *honor,* which is a contemporary synonym for *chivalry,* a concept that summons memories of the code of conduct for the knights of the Middle Ages in Europe. "*Honor* demands a certain amount of fairness in offense and defense and a certain mutual respect between opposing forces."[16]

---

15. This principle precludes the use of civilians and other protected persons and objects for military purposes. Today's military also recognizes in connection with this principle that the practice of some adversaries to mingle civilians with military personnel or fail to distinguish between the two may, in practice, make it hard to avoid incidental harm to civilians even though the obligation to the principle of noncombatant immunity remains an obligation. Ibid., 2.5.3.3; 2.5.5.

16. Ibid., 2.6.

It is important to note that the purpose of just war thinking in the history of Western thought was to make it difficult to decide for war. To declare a war just by these criteria is not to say it is good or right; it is to say that this tragic choice is the most ethically responsible course of action in this particular situation of our imperfect and broken world. The tragic character of that decision is perhaps no more deeply felt than by those who must go to war and send warriors into harm's way.

The ability to embrace some form of just war thinking will be essential to the chaplain's capacity for service as well as for their leadership in the formulation, promotion, and instruction of military ethics incumbent on all in service. However, for the chaplain there is a prior and more fundamental question. What is the theological justification of just war theory?

It hardly needs saying that people of faith, certainly in the Christian tradition, are united in their belief that the world is a place in which sin abounds. There is plenty of empirical evidence of evil to convince the religious and nonreligious alike that cruelty, violence, dishonesty, greed, corruption, and neglect are a constant throughout human history. How then do people of faith understand the task of ethics theologically in the context of this broken and frequently violent world? Just war theory says that the ethical task in this context requires of us to make the best choices possible consistent with the common good even when there are no perfectly good choices. And, as we shall see, military ethics, like other areas of applied ethics, as it faces specific decisions in its day-to-day operations, must function in ambiguous circumstances in which proximate values may be the best attainable. Christians would say that where sin abounds also grace abounds. This is the belief that by God's grace we are affirmed and empowered to be engaged in this messy world to seek those values that express love of neighbor and bear witness to God's will for peace and the flourishing of life.

Pacifists also believe that the world is a sinful place and that we have a duty in love for neighbor to care about the well-being of those in need or those who are suffering. They are equally as realistic as adherents to just war thinking. However, pacifists do not believe that our divine call to serve justice and the common good includes participation in violence even when it is inescapable and directed toward a good end. Both just war theorists and pacifists are committed to peacemaking. (We shall be taking up the subject of just peacemaking in chapter 9.) Pacifists see only nonviolent means as acceptable for the resolution of conflict.[17] Though pacifism is a minority

17. For a concise account of pacifism, see Hoekema, "A Practical Christian Pacifism," 917–919.

position it is an important and often courageous witness that needs to be noted. However, its premises obviously make it incompatible with the task of developing a military ethics for the day-to-day operations and mission of the armed services. For those who favor just war tradition we offer this twofold proposition to be taken up later.

> If *jus ad bellum* cannot be ethically justified there is no ground for jus in bello and the further ethical implications of its provisions. At the same time the failure of jus in bello in a given conflict can undermine the validity of just war claims based on the principles of *jus ad bellum*.

Even if one accepts the framework of just war theory for the development of military ethics that is not the end of the story. All ethical principles must be applied in context, which means that interpretation and judgments must be made. Situations may arise when specific actions in the conduct of war will appear to some to violate *jus in bello* or at least raise agonizing questions regarding its morality. A given war itself may be judged unjust. Obedience to command is an expectation and requirement of military life. It is a promise one makes upon entering military service. When a command or a mission in any activity of military life is judged to be unethical there is a serious ethical conflict. For persons whose understanding of military ethics is undergirded by the values and precepts of their faith this is a conflict between the ethical principle of promise-keeping (a sworn commitment to the state to obey orders) and another norm whose violation is a betrayal of one's faith, a species of conflict between God and country.[18] Chaplains are susceptible to such struggles of conscience, they are called to minister to those who feel deeply conflicted, and they have a responsibility to help commanders sort out and deal with ethical conflicts. Service members are not expected to obey illegal orders and should not, but even here there will sometimes be room for interpretation and, more importantly, legal orders can be given in what someone may judge to be an unjust cause. Dilemmas of this sort will be taken up later when we offer a proposed approach to

---

18. Eberle, in a lengthy article arising from his experience teaching at the United States Naval Academy, has argued that "theists," people of religious faith, cannot commit to indiscriminate obedience, including obedience to legal orders in an unjust cause since obedience to God always transcends obedience to government. Officer candidates who hold such belief should not take the Oath of Commissioning unless they can somehow understand that oath to be valid only for just causes. "God, War, and Conscience."

military ethics that we commend for chaplains in the exercise of their duties to service members and their commanders.

Chapter Three

Character and Virtues: The Warrior and the Chaplain

IT IS A COMMON understanding among ethicists that character and the virtues that express it are formed in a community shaped by a peculiar story. When we speak of character and the virtues it displays we are talking about the ethics of *being*, the sorts of persons we are, our disposition toward certain values that define our moral outlook and guide our behavior. Another way to think about the character of persons shaped by story-formed community is to understand them as participants in a culture determined by a critical set of experiences and challenges often but not always in dialectical relationship with religious beliefs. A culture ". . . comprises language, habits, ideas, beliefs, customs, social organization, inherited artifacts, technical processes, and values."[1] In our global society we are keenly aware of the vast variety of cultures and the conflicts that arise out of the frictions of diversity. In our own United States we have a multicultural society and at times like political campaigns we are continually made aware of the fact that culturally identifiable groups within our country have decidedly different perspectives on certain matters of public interest. However, it is not only ethnically specific groups or specifically religious groups whose narratives are sources of character formation. Medicine, for example, involves a professional community whose character in specific ways is dictated by a story of the fight against disease and death. It is a narrative that can lead some its practitioners to heights of devotion and self-sacrifice and it demands clear patterns of discipline in its ministry to the sick, injured, and dying. The military is no less a community with its own story-formed culture.

---

1. Niebuhr, *Christ and Culture*, 32.

Character and the Warrior Culture

Abraham Lincoln was correct when he said, "Character is like a tree, and reputation is like its shadow. The shadow is what we think of; the tree is the real thing." Character, like so many English words, reminds us of the ambiguous nature of language. Defining character is heavily dependent upon the context in which it is used as it clearly is in the context of military life. The US Army, US Navy, US Marine Corps, US Air Force, and US Coast Guard have statements regarding what the Army calls "Army Values" and the other services name "Core Values."

The US Army lists seven values it considers to be essential to the character of a soldier: loyalty, duty, respect, selfless service, honor, integrity, and personal courage. (In the context of the military what are called "values" are in the discourse of ethics generally understood as "virtues" and will be treated in those terms as the discussion proceeds.) For the Army the seven values begin with loyalty and are grounded in the Oath of Enlistment for enlisted personnel and in the Commissioning Oath for commissioned officers. True faith and allegiance to the Constitution of the United States is the bedrock upon which all other loyalty is built. Loyalty to leadership, loyalty to the unit, and loyalty to fellow soldiers all stem from the sworn allegiance to the Constitution. While the other uniformed services pare down the Army's list to three values (honor, courage, and commitment), they reflect the same essential characteristics. The theme of the core values throughout each of the uniformed services begins with loyalty to the Constitution of the United States, includes the courage to stand for the ideals embedded within the Constitution, and upholds the need for selfless dedication to the Constitution, the unit, and the individuals who make up the cadre of comrades in arms.

Out of these core values arises a narrative that in turn gives birth to a personal identity as a warrior. This narrative gives each individual member of the armed services an identity which is then shaped by the particular service branch into a form which matches the ethos of that particular warrior culture. Uniforms, customs, heroes, and traditions all contribute to the unique cultural identity of the individual warrior. Indeed, one of the fundamental goals of military basic training is to provide the process by which women and men enter as civilians and exit as soldiers. In this process civilian individuals shed their individuality and become integral members of a unit. Basic training takes the individual to new levels of physical fitness and mental discipline. Basic training instills pride through mastering the proper way to wear a uniform, overcoming difficult circumstances, and managing one's mental outlook. Basic training brings individuals into a closed community forged through shared hardship and mutual effort with other recruits. Basic training creates bonds between individuals by stressing teamwork in an atmosphere of living, working, training, and learning together without regard for individual differences under a regimen of shared rules. Basic training teaches recruits to discard their individuality for the sake of accomplishing the mission and in so doing they are formed into a team. Basic training instills within the individual the ability to understand and execute verbal commands without the need for reflection because someday those immediate responses may save another soldier's life. The basic training experience transforms individuals from civilians into warriors without which no military can exist and creates a common experience that nearly every veteran looks back upon with unspoken pride. Basic training, the crucible experience of every warrior, is the place where the narrative that shapes the warrior identity begins.

Unless a chaplain has had prior military enlisted or officer service it is unlikely that the chaplain has had the transformational experience of basic training. Chaplain corps officers receive direct appointments as officers or as Chaplain Candidate Program Officers when they enter military service. Chaplains do complete a Basic Chaplain Corps Officer course of approximately eight weeks in duration.

From the Personal History of Wollom Jensen

My personal experience of going to war occurred as it does for most young men and women at age nineteen. Following two academically disastrous semesters at university I decided that I needed to do something that would help me gain a sense of personal discipline in my life. I knew that I had always felt an attraction to military life but I also knew that while I had often dreamt of being a military officer I was not yet ready for that responsibility. So in the summer of 1967 I volunteered for the draft and soon found myself on the way to basic training in August of that year.

Basic training was a physically, emotionally, and (while not as clear to me at the time) spiritually challenging experience. The discipline, regimentation, and environment provided me with the structure I had felt was missing in my life.

I was made a squad leader during the first week of basic training mostly as a result of the ROTC training I had participated in during that first academically failed year. The second day of basic training we were instructed by our senior drill instructor that we were to call out "Attention" when a commissioned officer entered our barracks. Likewise, when an NCO (Noncommissioned Officer) entered we were to call out "At Ease!" Following that brief period of instruction, Senior Drill Sergeant Hayes left. He returned to the barracks unannounced barely five minutes later. I was standing near my bunk with a clear view of the door. I saw the senior drill sergeant enter and called out loudly, "At Ease!" The first words out of Senior Drill Sergeant Hayes mouth were, "God-damn-it! Who said At Ease?" My heart raced, my stomach emptied, and my mouth went dry. I feared what was about to come. Somewhat timidly I managed to say, "I did, Senior Drill Sergeant"

The whole barracks fell silent and I was the recipient of some furtive glances from my fellow trainees while the senior drill sergeant bore holes in me with his squinted eyes as he marched purposefully toward me. When he finally reached me he stood toe-to-toe, nose-to-nose with me and starred unblinkingly into my eyes.

"Who told you to call At Ease?" he growled.

"You did Senior Drill Sergeant Hayes" I replied quietly.

"God-damn it, Jensen. You're the only swinging dick in this whole God damned mob who apparently listens to instruction. Here are your corporal stripes. You are now a squad leader."

This was the first and perhaps most important lesson I learned in basic training. Listen, understand, and obey all orders. Everything else in the warrior culture is built upon this building block. Do not think about, analyze, or second-guess a command, simply obey it. In the fog and haze of the emotional stress and sensory overload created by in the basic training environment one gets a sense of the fog and haze of war. In combat your life and the lives of your fellow soldiers depends upon everyone doing what is ordered and doing it immediately. Critical analysis and reflection can come later in a debriefing once the situation has been resolved.

Respect for and confidence in authority is one of the essential characteristics of a warrior. This implies that a leader of warriors, one who gives commands, must be worthy of the respect and confidence placed in him or her. One of the questions warriors often pose to themselves is, "Would I want to go to war with this commander?" It is a question that speaks to the character of the other. Does the person possess those qualities of courage, honor, endurance, self-discipline, competence, judgment, and compassion that allows the warrior to know that he will not be wasted, forgotten, or left on the battlefield?

Everything incorporated into the teaching plan for basic trainees is focused upon making warriors out of civilians. There is a huge effort to stifle individuality and to foster a sense of unit cohesion. Little sleep and a lot of arduous physical training help to challenge the limits of physical endurance and help the trainee to learn that your body can do much more than your mind, whose job it is to protect your body, thinks it can. Stress and psychological pressure teaches the trainee to cope with the stress of battle and to develop the ability to think clearly under pressure by assessing the situation and learning to rapidly set priorities. Endless inspections of weapons, uniforms, beds, and barracks teach the recruits not only the importance of paying attention to detail, but how to pay attention to details.

Hours are spent on the rifle range, in hand-to-hand combat training, and at the bayonet course. This training not only teaches the applicable techniques and skills of using weapons but also helps to set the mind-set necessary for war.

"What's the Spirit of the Bayonet, Company?" the drill sergeants would shout.

"To KILL, Drill Sergeant!" the company would respond.

"What are the two types of bayonet fighters, Company?" the drill sergeants would respond.

"The quick and the dead, drill sergeant!" we would shout back in reply.

Then we would be off to impale with our bayonet and butt stroke with our weapon the dummies that lined the bayonet course.

When quizzed by Professor Shannon French in a philosophy class at the United States Naval Academy regarding the meaning of the word "warrior," Professor French prompted the Midshipmen with words such as killer, fighter, murderer, victor, and conquerer. The Midshipmen responded in earnest and often impassioned ways to the words suggested by Professor French. The Midshipmen averred that there is a difference between a true warrior and a combatant.

Why did the Midshipmen react in such animated ways? For the same reason that the military places such a high emphasis upon the notion of character and a developed set of core values. The Midshipmen, like their counterparts at the United States Military Academy, the United States Air Force Academy, and the United States Coast Guard Academy, are preparing to become commissioned officers in the armed services of the United States. These young men and women are preparing themselves to be professional military leaders of other young men and women who will also serve in the armed services of the United States. As such these young men and women will be sent into harm's way where they will be expected to carry out the orders and accomplish the missions given to them ultimately by the commander-in-chief, the president of the United States, on behalf of the nation. Succinctly, these young Midshipmen and Cadets will lead other young men and women in kinetic connectivity, i.e. in armed combat where they will see, hear, smell, taste, and experience the basest behaviors known to humankind. In these situations not only will these young men and women risk their own lives and limbs, but they will be asked to take the lives of other combatants in battle. They will not only be asked to make the ultimate sacrifice on behalf of the nation but they will be asked to bear the physical, psychological, and moral (or perhaps more accurately) soul wounds which inevitably come as a result of war. Of all the wounds suffered in battle these moral or soul wounds perhaps have the most devastating impact upon the warrior.

Warriors are asked not only to be witnesses to the basest of human behaviors; they are asked to be active participants. Killing, maiming, psychological and emotional pain are expected, encouraged, and demanded by kinetic contact with the enemy. While much has been written about the warrior experience perhaps none more accurately captures the experience than Karl Marlantes. Marlantes writes, "The Marine Corps taught me how to kill but it didn't teach me how to deal with killing."[2]

When I was a student at the Lutheran Theological Seminary in Gettysburg, Pennsylvania, I often walked south from the campus along Seminary Ridge Road until I arrived at the spot from which Confederate Major General George Pickett launched his charge against the center of the Union lines. I have stood in the woods on Seminary Ridge and looked across the vast expanse leading up to the monument marking the "high-water mark" of the Confederate assault. I've walked the distance from Seminary Ridge to the "high-water mark" monument and have pondered what it took for the men of Pickett's division to make that assault. Standing in the relative safety of the tree line on Seminary Ridge, I have asked myself and others, "What would make these men leave this ridge and move forward against that far distant Union line?" The answer that I arrived at is the one many others have also come to—honor. No soldier wants to let the soldier to the left or right down.

2. Marlantes, What It Is Like to Go to War, 3.

They all depend upon each other to do their best and thereby insuring the greatest likelihood of success. They handed each other letters to be sent home in the case of their death. They promised each other that each would do his utmost to insure that no one was left alone on the battlefield whether dead or alive. From this important value arose the other values of courage, commitment, integrity, selfless service, and sacrifice. These core warrior values are ultimately rooted in trustworthiness.

The core warrior values can, perhaps, be summed up in one word: character. But why the emphasis upon core warrior values and character? Character is so important within the military that we can see its reflection within military law. An officer may be brought before a court marital on the charge of adultery, for instance. An officer may be disciplined for conduct unbecoming an officer. These offenses are but a few examples of the emphasis upon character within the warrior community. But why is character so important in a warrior culture? There are two main reasons.

First, warriors must be able to trust each other for their lives depend upon it. Each warrior must have complete confidence in the others' *trustworthiness. Courage, honor, commitment, professionalism, and self-sacrifice are all different facets of trustworthiness.*

Second, the civilian population also depends upon the warrior being of good character. In the tradition of just war during the conduct of a war, "jus in bello," a warrior is asked to participate in the killing, maiming, and destruction of property in pursuit of defeating the enemy on behalf of the nation. However, the ethical demand for loving-kindness toward one's neighbor, demands that there be some controls regarding a warrior's behavior in battle. Wholesale violence and unrestrained killing becomes nothing more than murder and wanton destruction. Equally important is the concern for fellow citizens back home. It is anticipated that warriors will return home and will reenter the civilian life at some point. What has become expected of the warrior on the battlefield must be set aside upon returning to civilian life. The behaviors that contributed to success on the battlefield are unacceptable in the home community. Just as there was a period of transition from civilian into warrior, so there must be a period of transition out of the warrior role and back into the civilian role. Again, character rises to the forefront. Fellow citizens must be able to count on a returned warrior to reintegrate into the standards of behavior of the civilian population.

Consider the character of a warrior chaplain. The women and men who have discerned first a call to the ordained ministry have also discerned a call to serve the women and men of the armed forces at home and abroad. They have, for the sake of service, accepted and adopted the character the warrior while yet maintaining the essence of the call of Jesus within their person; that by no standard of measure is an easy task. Matthew 5:48 reads, "You, therefore, must be perfect, as your heavenly Father is perfect." Here we find both the bane and the blessing of service as a military chaplain.

Christian military chaplains are faced with the daunting challenge of living in two worlds. They live in the world of the warrior and they live within the world of their non-warrior faith communities. This is a difficult place for Christian clergy to live. While they must adapt to and become part of the warrior community, Christian chaplains must never lose sight of the reality that they are noncombatants. While their warrior counterparts are given the sword to wield on behalf of the nation, Christian chaplains are neither given nor must they take up the sword. While others such as physicians may take up the sword in defense of others, Christian chaplains may not.

To those serving as warriors within the military, Christian military chaplains represent not only their faith communities, they also represent Christ. They are there to serve others in humility and self-giving love. This means that they care not only for their own, but they must care for all, including their enemies. Within the American military chaplains are normally assigned an enlisted person who is a warrior and who is armed and trained in the use of weapons. It is frequently said that the chaplain's assistant is there to protect the chaplain but this is problematical for the Christian chaplain. The protection of a chaplain's life is not consistent with the call to be a representative of Christ. Jesus said, in the garden on the night of his arrest, "Peter, put away your sword" (John 18:11). He who could summon St. Michael and all angels the to protect him did not do so for his life was not taken from him but laid down by him in obedience to his Father.

There are stories of chaplains picking up weapons in the heat of battle to fight off the enemy. These actions are often justified by asserting that it was a last defense by the chaplain of his or her comrades, if not him or herself. While this may appear honorable at first blush, those same soldiers reported that in those instances when their chaplain picked up a weapon they lost hope. It can also be argued that once a chaplain has used a weapon in combat his or her ordination has become irregular and that chaplain must of necessity be barred from presiding at the Eucharist because of it. The chaplain is no longer able to represent Christ, the one who gave himself up for the sake of all others. This is a very heavy burden and one which requires courage, commitment, honor, and obedience that can only arise out of a deep and abiding sense of call to the life of *agape* in loving service to others.

The character of a Christian military chaplain cannot be of one's own making. It must be rooted in baptism and shaped by the promise of the One who gave himself up on behalf of others and with whom we died and were raised in the waters of baptism. As St. Paul said, "We do not live to ourselves, and we do not die to ourselves. If we live, we life to the Lord, and if we die, we die to the Lord; so then, whether we live or whether we die, we are the Lord's" (Rom 14:7–8).

Character and the "Warrior" Chaplain: Living in Two Worlds

The story of the chaplain's faith community that shapes the character of its members is the narrative of God's self-disclosure in history. That narrative, which shapes the faith and life of the community, is understood to be the ultimate framework of meaning. It is the ultimate truth of reality within which are fitted and judged all other stories of communities in which the faithful are engaged. Since the community's narrative is given by God as divine self-disclosure, its very logic is that it is universal and supercedes and norms all other influences on character. Thus, the cultures born of the various narratives in which people of faith participate are examined or should be examined through the lens of that overarching ultimate narrative. How then does the character of the chaplain, formed by faith and *the* faith, interact with the character expectations of the military culture? How do the virtues expressive of the character of these two worlds relate to one another? If formation in one's faith is paramount in what respect can the chaplain embrace the values inherent in the military culture? These are the questions we must now address. [3]

---

3. Peter French has described this as the "two collar" conflict facing military chaplains: "On the right collar is the insignia of military rank. On the left collar is the insignia of the chaplain's faith—a cross, tablet, a crescent, or a Dharmacakra. At virtually every PDTC [professional development training course] at least one chaplain would point to his two collars during the discussion of an ethical issue related to some military situation that struck very near to home. That action was the universal symbol in the Corps that expressed the schizophrenic nature of their jobs." *War and Moral Dissonance*, 10.

Formed by Love

As stated above, the chaplain's call as a noncombatant among warriors "requires courage, commitment, honor, and obedience that can only arise out of a deep and abiding sense of call to the life of *agape* in loving service to others." The chaplain as one called out of the Christian community for his/ her special ministry shares with others of the community that character of love formed by grace in the image of the Christ: "And all of us, with unveiled faces, seeing the glory of the Lord as though reflected in a mirror, are being transformed into the same image from one degree of glory to another; for this comes from the Lord, the Spirit" (2 Cor 3:18).

In the Genesis 2 narrative of creation God is portrayed in the likeness of a potter shaping humanity from the dust of the earth and breathing life into it. By analogy the character of *agape* love is shaped and brought to life from the dust of human sin and finitude by God's transforming love revealed in Christ. We are to love as we have been loved: "I give you a new commandment, that you love one another. Just as I have loved you, you also should love one another" (John 13:34). What, then, does that *agape* love entail?[4]

First and foremost, this *agape*, this neighbor love, is in its outlook *universal* or *all-inclusive*. No one is excluded from love's concern. Matthew 5:43–44 is a critical passage in this regard for it is here that Jesus commands his followers to love even their enemies and bless those who persecute them. Difficult as this may seem and actually is, it reflects the pattern of God's love, as Matthew 5:45 goes on to say: "He makes his sun to rise on the evil and on the good, and sends rain on the righteous and on the unrighteous." And one cannot fail to recall the universal scope of John 3:16, which proclaims God's love for the entire world (the Greek is *cosmos*). The implication is that the outreach of Christian love is to all without exception. "Isms" like racism, sexism, and classism, etc., are out of the question. Loving is not the same as liking; it is not only the likeable who are the object of our love. This is the unconditional nature of neighbor love from which no one is disqualified.

One implication of *agape*'s universality of outlook for the character and conduct of chaplains in the Christian tradition is the acceptance and readiness to serve all without prejudice and to regard all as people whom God loves. It demands the ability in theology and practice to defer judgment

---

4. See the discussion of *agape* in Childs, *Ethics in the Community of Promise*, 35–43.

of others to God's mercy. One important implication of this point we have already touched upon is the readiness to minister to all in a pluralistic situation.

Another way to unpack *agape's* universality of care is to emphasize that an ethic grounded in neighbor love cannot practice *exclusivism*. We have met confessional exclusivism in the previous chapter. Here we speak of exclusivism in slightly different terms. We speak of "ethical exclusivism," which occurs when we regard a particular group of people as somehow less than fully human in the sense that they are excluded from the same consideration of rights and needs that others deserve. In this view we do not owe them the same ethical obligations as we do to others. Historically, Native Americans in being dispossessed and African Americans during enslavement and beyond have been treated as those essentially without equal rights. Environmentalists would tend to argue that human beings have often disregarded the biotic rights of other creatures. These are all expressions of ethical exclusivism.

So also, in situations of armed conflict it is easy for the enemy to become demonized and regarded as outside the pale of humane considerations. Acts of brutality and cruelty evoke the understandable exclusivist response that the enemy has thereby abdicated any of the intrinsic value that we would normally accord to other human beings. The Geneva Conventions and rules of engagement designed to preserve *jus in bello,* along with other documents, are in place to deal with this very phenomenon.[5] Laws and rules can often compel compliance when backed by sufficiently harsh penalties but they do not create commitment. The chaplain is called to embody in spirituality and practice the commitment to love's equal regard for the value of all persons, even those guilty of heinous acts in the heat of battle or in the atrocities of terrorism.

The chaplain is no less susceptible to feelings of hatred and rage toward those whose lethal hatred has been visited upon his/her comrades. But, through constant prayer and immersion in the means of grace the chaplain can seek the power in some real way to continue to love one's

---

5. "Through the mechanisms of the Hague and the Geneva Conventions, the Charter of the United Nations, military manuals such as the United States Army's *Law of Land Warfare,* and similar documents, modern governments and militaries attempt to distinguish 'just war' and just conduct in war from other types of killing of human beings. Morally conscientious military personnel need to understand and frame their actions in moral terms so as to maintain moral integrity in the midst of the actions and stress of combat." Cook, *The Moral Warrior,* 21.

enemy as Christ commands. This means recognizing in tangible ways that, though one must kill those who menace the lives of others, it is tragic. It is not a cause for rejoicing or the heady satisfaction of revenge. Only then can the chaplain minister to others who must do the killing and bear the burden of conscience that so often follows. Recall the comment by Karl Marlantes, "The Marine Corps taught me how to kill but it didn't teach me how to deal with killing." Recall also the earlier observation that when a chaplain picks up a weapon the soldiers lose hope.

Can one really fulfill Jesus' command to love one's enemies and so fulfill the universality or unconditional nature of *agape*? It can be hard for chaplains even as noncombatants committed to the love ethic. Given the nature of the combat situation is it even conceivable for warriors, if not absurd? The war movies I watched as a child during World War II certainly caricatured the enemy soldiers as the embodiment of evil. Their destruction brought cheers in the darkened theater. The media has often played to our human propensities to relish revenge. Programs like *M.A.S.H.*, with its skillful blend of humor and reality, have helped us to a more nuanced and humane understanding of the reality of war, but the advent of terrorism and 9/11 has brought back some of that capacity for hatred.

It may in fact be the case that warriors with a code of respect for their ·enemy warriors have a tradition for "love of enemy," however modified by the tragic conditions of warfare, that surpasses some our more chauvinistic civilians.[6] To the extent that this tradition has held sway is it now compromised by the nature of combat in the face of barbarian terrorist tactics by combatants who are not the servants of their state? Or, how are we to gain a sense of fellow feeling for the enemy in the sterile world of drone warfare? These are crucial questions for the military in general and for chaplains as spiritual leaders, in particular. Yet, even under the conditions of present-day warfare, the reality of our co-humanity with our enemies still confronts us.

The case of Lt. Col. Stuart Couch, the Marine lawyer who refused to prosecute a suspect at Guantanamo because he was convinced that the man had been tortured, is worth mentioning at this junction in our discussion. Lt. Col. Couch was a member of several communities: his Christian faith community, his national community as a loyal American citizen, his Marine community, his legal professional community, marriage and family,

---

6. As previously noted, the concept of honor is discussed in the DOD *Law of War Manual*, 2.6.

close friends and colleagues from his days as a pilot. He was strongly committed to the values entailed in these various communities. In his circle of friends from flying days was the first officer of the plane that was crashed by terrorists into the South Tower of the World Trade Center on 9/11. When he began his duties as a prosecutor of terrorists he kept a picture of his fallen colleague's wife and children on his desk. Couch's desire to prosecute the terrorist in question was born of his belief that this terrorist had the most blood on his hands. When evidence of torture became apparent with the prisoner's sudden readiness to cooperate, Couch was conflicted as one can well imagine, given the multiple narratives shaping his character. Reportedly, what clinched his decision to refuse to prosecute was further knowledge of coercive tactics coupled with the priest's question to the congregants in the course of a baptismal ritual as to whether they were committed to respect the dignity of every human being.[7] In Couch's case the capacity to love one's enemy found expression in a courageous act to insist on respect for the dignity of all despite evidence of guilt. Perhaps one may hazard the conclusion that in this particular case the Christian story was large enough to encompass and illuminate the narratives of all the other communities.

The eminent theologian Jürgen Moltmann shares a very different but also instructive example of love for the enemy. Moltmann came from a secular background in which Goethe and Nietzsche were his heroes until his service in the German army during World War II. He was overwhelmed by its catastrophic proportions of mass death and by his guilt over why he survived and not others, like the schoolmate who was blown to pieces by a bomb while standing next to him. While a prisoner of war in Scotland from 1945–1948 he came to faith. What he describes as a "well-meaning Army chaplain" gave him a Bible. In the Bible he discovered in Jesus' cry from the cross, "My, my God, why have you forsaken me?"—a God who suffered with us.[8] Adjunct to his coming to faith was his experience of the kindness of his captors:

> The kindness which Scottish miners and English neighbors showed the German prisoners of war who were at the time their

7. This account is recorded by Eric Mount, "Terrorism, Torture, and Conscience." Mount goes on to caution the reader that though Couch's faith seemed decisive in this case, a Pew survey in 2005 showed that secular Americans are more likely to oppose torture than Protestants and Catholics!

8. Moltmann, *In the End—The Beginning*, 34–35.

enemies shamed us profoundly. We were accepted as people, even though we were only numbers and wore the prisoner's patch on our backs. But that made it possible for us to live with the guilt of our people, the catastrophes we had brought about and the long shadows of Auschwitz, without repressing them and without becoming callous.[9]

Moltmann's memories and reflections on the outreach of the chaplain and the kindness of his captors demonstrate the capacity of people to distinguish between the intrinsic value of each human being from the tragic circumstances which have made them their enemy. Stories like this and that of Col. Couch are the stories of *the Story*. They belong in the portfolio of every Christian and every chaplain working hard at the reality and possibility of *agape* love's unconditional outreach.

Second, the character of *agape* love is self-giving. It entails for those called to lead the attitude of servant leadership. Servant leadership is an ethical demand for all military leadership and the chaplain has the vocation to embody and promote it. How it plays itself out in the conduct of commissioned and noncommissioned officers will be the subject of our later discussion of the ethical norm of respect for autonomy. For the present we are focused on this dimension of *agape* in the character formation of the chaplain.

The biblical injunction that Christian discipleship is service, *diakonia*, is spelled out for us in Matthew 20:25–28: "But Jesus called them to him and said, 'You know that the rulers of the Gentiles lord it over them, and their great ones are tyrants over them. It will not be so among you; but whoever wishes to be great among you must be your servant, and whoever wishes to be first among you must be your slave; just as the Son of Man came not to be served but to serve, and to give his life a ransom for many.'"

Obviously, the term *minister* means one who serves. What this call is all about is therefore not in the least bit ambiguous; it is a call to service written into the very demands of the vocational job description. Notwithstanding that, ministers of all sorts, including chaplains, are sinful human beings like all people and are not always above self-centered considerations of self-preservation and self-promotion that can get in the way of servanthood. As in all occupations of leadership one wants to do one's best and to be recognized for it in some tangible and meaningful way. The key to servant leadership is to see one's success in terms of the values it has

9. Ibid., 35.

provided for the needs of those being served rather than simply in terms of self-aggrandizement.

Chaplains, like all leaders, have the well-being of others entrusted to their care. The officers they serve have the lives of their personnel entrusted to them. It is critical in both cases that this kind of leadership is clearly seen as involving a sacred trust. It is an entailment of love's commitment to the sanctity of life. And in that capacity the self-giving character of servant-hood in chaplaincy finds concrete expression in that those who accept this vocation give up certain prerogatives of freedom that clergy outside the military enjoy. They are always on duty with those entrusted to their care, with their warriors at all times, sharing with them those times when there is no haven of rest or safety.

The commitment to servant leadership as an expression of *agape's* self-giving orientation of character involves a Christlike spirituality. So it is that Paul invoked the great christological hymn recorded in his admonition to the Philippians and to us:

> Let each of you look not to your own interests, but to the interests of others. Let the same mind be in you that was in Christ Jesus, who, though he was in the form of God, did not regard equality with God as something to be exploited, but emptied himself, taking the form of a slave, being born in human likeness. And being found in human form, he humbled himself and became obedient to the point of death—even death on a cross. Therefore God also highly exalted him and gave him the name that is above every name, so that at the name of Jesus every knee should bend, in heaven and on earth and under the earth, and every tongue should confess that Jesus Christ is Lord, to the glory of God the Father (Phil. 2:4–11).

The spirit of the Christ that Paul commended was echoed in Martin Luther's famous "theology of the cross." In 1518, less than a year after the posting of the ninety-five theses, Luther engaged his critics in the Disputation at Heidelberg. The following theses underlie what became to be known as his theology of the cross:

"18. It is certain that [one} must utterly despair of his or her own ability before they are prepared to receive the grace of Christ.

19. That person does not deserve to be called a theologian who looks upon the invisible things of God as though they were clearly perceptible in those things that have actually happened.

20. He or she deserves to be called a theologian, however, who comprehends visible and manifest things of God seen through the suffering of the cross.

[*Then the famous one:*]

21. A theology of glory calls evil good and good evil. A theology of the cross calls the thing what it actually is.

22. That wisdom which sees the invisible things of God in works as perceived by people is completely puffed up, blinded and hardened."[10]

The target of these theses in the ecclesiastical context of Luther's day was the arrogant presumption of an authoritarian church leadership that claimed absolute truth for its teachings. Moreover these theologians of glory, Luther believed, were distorting the gospel by prescribing burdensome and false works needed for salvation. For theologians of the cross who have seen the truth of their own brokenness in the brutal reality of the crucified, there could be no such pretense regarding one's infallibility or ability to contribute to one's salvation. The corollary of the theology of the cross is the central theme of the Reformation: justification by grace through faith.

The theology of the cross as a consequence conveys a spirituality of humility. Douglas John Hall has captured this nicely:

> The *theologia gloria* confuses and distorts because it presents divine revelation in a straightforward, undialectical, and authoritarian manner that silences doubt—silences therefore real humanity. It overwhelms the human with its brilliance, its incontestability, its certitude. Yet just in this it confuses and distorts, because God's object in the divine self-manifestation is precisely not to overwhelm but to befriend.[11]

The spirituality of the cross is incumbent on all faithful Christian leaders but for military chaplains there is a special urgency to cultivate a genuine sense of humility in one's own spiritual life, not simply as a pose. The chaplain's spirituality teaches and inspires by example; the spirituality of the cross reveals a faith reliant on God's grace and mercy. What could be more essential to the spiritual well-being of those embroiled in the terrors of war and the terrors of conscience it may bring?

10. Luther, "Heidelberg Disputation," 40–41.
11. Hall, *The Cross in Our Context*, 20.

The theology and spirituality of the cross is foundational to the ethics of love functioning in a world of radical moral ambiguity.

To appreciate the truth of the cross in one's own life and one's total reliance on the grace of God is essential to those who minister in the midst of war's tragic ambiguity surrounded by warriors of all faiths or no faith, who at any time in the heat of conflict or the remorse of its aftermath may need a ministry of compassion and not judgments born of moral superiority. Indeed compassion is a dimension of *agape*'s character of servanthood. It is the ability to take the suffering of the other into oneself, a sense of deep solidarity. In the accounts of Jesus' feeding miracles it is said that when he saw the crowd that had followed him and their deep need, he had "compassion" on them (Matt 14:14, Mark 6:34). The Greek word behind "compassion" is strong; it means a going out of one's very "guts" to those in need. It prefigures one might suggest the ultimate giving of self—body and soul—in the crucifixion.

A pause for a check on reality is in order before we proceed further, however. The pouring out of oneself in concern for the other at the heart of compassion can for mere mortals bearing the burden of caring may come up against its limits. We speak of compassion fatigue. Compassion fatigue is a condition, sometimes referred to as Secondary Traumatic Stress, often experienced by caregivers who work with victims of trauma. It is generally characterized by a gradual lessening of compassion over time. While certainly not unique to military chaplains (in fact it was first diagnosed in the 1950s among nurses), compassion fatigue has become a significant reality among military chaplains who have served or are serving in combat environments.

In the wake of twelve years of ongoing war, the longest in US History, military chaplains are suffering the wounds of war including spiritual, moral, physical, and psychological wounds. With multiple deployments like their combatant brothers- and sisters-in-arms, military chaplains are tired, and often spiritually depleted from their experiences of caring for troops who bear the brunt of the burden of kinetic engagements.

In addition to providing pastoral care for those who are wounded, military chaplains are also responsible for providing pastoral care to the medical staff, other support personnel, combat commanders who are charged with the responsibilities of leading warriors into battle, to civilians caught in the fray, and to wounded enemy soldiers. In providing this demanding and broad-ranging pastoral care to the men and women serving in combat units military, chaplains are exposed over and over again to the devastating effects of war. These circumstances demand from military chaplains not only their compassionate pastoral skills but also their most deeply held ethical convictions. Living in a near constant state of fear, hypervigilance, and high demand for pastoral skills, the military chaplain must also contend with his or her own sense of separation from things familiar such as family, home, and religious community. In these trying circumstances the military chaplain is frequently seen as the bearer of hope to the combat troops.

A bearer is a person who presents or upholds something. In this context, a military chaplain presents or upholds hope for those conducting combat operations. It is almost a tautology to say that in order to be a bearer of hope the military chaplain must also be a possessor of hope. The hope that the chaplain brings to the troops wells up from within his/her own faith-born hope. Only then can it bring hope to others.

In the midst of combat, a world which shows humankind at its basest and most broken state, it is not uncommon for soldiers to lose their hope that there is any meaning in their actions. People are hurt, maimed, and killed, while others are hurting, maiming, and killing, and all around the value of human life is diminished. The lines of demarcation between the quick and the dead while stark are also blurred in the eyes of those who are engaged in heavy combat, just as the differentiation between the good and the evil are obliterated.

Compassion fatigue is one of the spiritual wounds suffered by military chaplains serving and caring for the needs of warriors within an active combat area of operations. Indeed, it might well be argued that compassion fatigue is the most significant of spiritual wounds experienced by chaplains in combat. As men and women of faith military chaplains must be deeply rooted in their own faith traditions and communities. This rooting is essential in maintaining a healthy emotional and spiritual life while living in the place where demons dwell. However, more is needed for the military chaplain to be firmly planted and rooted in the rich soil of moral and ethical reflection and the hope born out of a faith commitment and tradition. There is a need for chaplains to receive compassionate support from others within the faith; not simply fellow chaplains but an enlightened church that appreciates the ministry they perform.

Third, the goal of God's love in Christ is, as Paul Tillich famously put it, the reunification of the separated.[12] This means bringing humanity back in right relationship with God and with each other in the human community. Dietrich Bonhoeffer put the matter this way: "The disunion of human beings from God, from other human beings, from the world and from themselves is ended. . . . Love thus denotes what God does to human beings to overcome the disunion in which they lived. This deed is called Christ, it is called reconciliation."[13]

> So if anyone is in Christ, there is a new creation: everything old has passed away; see, everything has become new! All this is from God, who reconciled us to himself through Christ, and has given us the ministry of reconciliation; that is, in Christ God was reconciling the world to himself, not counting their trespasses against them, and entrusting the message of reconciliation to us (2 Cor 5:17–19).

Divine forgiveness is love's power to heal the rifts of a fallen world. It is also the power to heal the deep divisions within our own souls. In Romans 7 the Apostle Paul struggles with the conflict within himself. "For I do not do what I want, but I do the very thing I hate" (v. 15). The answer he finds for deliverance from this conflict in the mercy of God in Christ. Surely this conflict, for the chaplain living in two worlds, is hardly unknown. As the healing power of God's forgiving, reconciling love makes its presence felt in his own internal conflicts, so will her capacity be nourished for ministry to the lesions within the spirit of warriors who find they must do "the very thing [they] hate."

But how is it possible to conceive of this reconciling dimension of love's character to seek unity in the midst of war with one's enemies? The following statement from a study on soldier spirituality done by Army Reserve Chaplain, Col. Franklin Eric Wester speaks directly to this question.

> While *esprit de corps* is important, it is vital for a Soldier to not just feel like she or he belongs to the unit but also belongs to the rest of the human race. Beyond a connection to others, even a generalized bond to humanity, spirituality regularly finds expression in religious activities . . . . Soldiers who integrate connection to others at a deep level of their humanity recognize even their enemies are still part of humanity deserving certain rights and protections. A

12. Tillich, *Sytematic Theology*, vol. 3, 95.

13. Bonhoeffer, *Ethics*, 335–336.

connection to others may mitigate enemy abuses, POW mistreatment, and civilian casualties.[14]

Ultimately, love's character embodies the relationship between love and justice. The spirituality of human solidarity Wester speaks of involves an internalized sense of justice. An orientation of character toward justice is an essential component of the internalization of love's goal of reconciliation. We are still speaking here of the character of love in the formation of the chaplain's spirituality as it relates to the character of the warrior the chaplain serves. Ultimately the relationship of love, justice, and reconciliation (the attainment and promotion of peace in the resolution of the conflict) at the political level involves serious reflection on the principles of just war to which we return later.

Meanwhile, the connection we have seen between love and justice provides us with a further opportunity to address the following question: *How can we see the character of military culture through the lens of love in such a way that the character of* agape *represents an ultimate truth that can encompass the penultimate realities of military character?*

Reinhold Niebuhr's discussion of justice and love speaks to this question and provides us with a paradigm for the chaplain's life in two worlds. Niebuhr distinguished between love and justice but did not separate them. This was an important step away from the sort of dichotomous thinking that relegated love to the personal behavior of the Christian while justice was the province of worldly authorities. For Niebuhr, the realist, justice is involved with the tragic choices that confront nations and leaders in a complex and conflictual world. Love tempers justice by its criticism of selfish claims enabling justice, in turn, to serve the purposes of love by its own ability to resist selfish claims. Without the critique of love, justice deteriorates into corruption and without the realism of justice, love, even though heroic to the point of martyrdom, cannot function amidst the constant challenges of effecting a harmonious society. "No possible historic justice is sufferable without the Christian hope. But any illusion of a world of perfect love without the imperfect harmonies of justice must ultimately turn the dream of love into a nightmare of tyranny and injustice."[15]

For Niebuhr, the Christian story with its central ethical principle of *agape* can encompass and give meaning and direction to the penultimate stories of entities engaged in the ambiguous and tragic choices of justice.

14. Wester, "'Soldier Spirituality.'"

15. Niebuhr, "Justice and Love," 29.

Justice in its manifold expressions, like just war principles, exists to protect the God-given value of all humanity and, as such, for all its imperfections, serves the goal of *agape*'s universality. At the same time, justice is necessary because in human perversity some will often seek to deny that God-given worth to others. Not surprisingly, Niebuhr was a critic of pacifism.

PART II

Virtues and Principles:
The Chaplain and the Warrior

IN THE CHAPTERS THAT follow we will unpack further the questions of love's character as it finds expression in certain virtues and principles. The discussion will continue to focus attention on the vocation and moral formation of the chaplain but also serve to point out how chaplains can correlate in their own understanding and for the sake of their ministry the virtues and principles of *agape* with those of the military culture. In so doing we will be laying the groundwork for the question of ethical method that will follow in Part III.

The seven core values of the US Army—loyalty, duty, respect, selfless service, honor, integrity, and personal courage—will serve as our model for the basic precepts of military ethics. A study of ethics education in the military by Paul Robinson of the University of Ottawa shows that these seven values are representative of a number of military services in other countries as well.[1] Though the Army refers to them as "values," we treat them as "virtues" involving "principles" that, once again, we want to look at through the lens of *agape* love.

In each of the next three chapters we will deal with two of the military core values, concluding with the virtue of honor as the overarching principle for the entire system. When we look at each of the values and the explanation given them in the official Army posting we can analyze them in "ethics speak" as follows: the values, loyalty, duty, etc. are basically general principles or general rules and the explanation of what each these

1. Robinson, "Introduction: Ethics Education in the Military," 7.

general rules entail is on the order of a "middle axiom," a principle more specific than the general rule but still requiring further interpretation in actual practice.

Chapter Four

Loyalty and Duty: A Matter of Promise-Keeping[1]

Loyalty:

Bear true faith and allegiance to the U.S. Constitution, the Army, your unit and other Soldiers. Bearing true faith and allegiance is a matter of believing in and devoting yourself to something o r someone. A loyal Soldier is one who supports the leadership and stands up for fellow Soldiers. By wearing the uniform of the U.S. Army you are expressing your loyalty. And by doing your share, you show your loyalty to your unit.

Duty:

Fulfill your obligations. Doing your duty means more than carrying out your assigned tasks. Duty means being able to accomplish tasks as part of a team. The work of the U.S. Army is a complex combination of missions, tasks and responsibilities—all in constant motion. Our work entails building one assignment onto another. You fulfill your obligations as a part of your unit every time you resist the temptation to take "shortcuts" that might undermine the integrity of the final product.

WE HAVE ALREADY SAID a great deal about the nature of *agape* love in which Christian character is formed after the image of the Christ. We have also noted a number of ways in which this formation has specific implications for the vocation and practice of military chaplaincy. However, more needs to be said in unpacking the virtues and principles in which we are

---

1. The Values and their explanations here and in the next two chapters are taken for the Army website, http://www.goarmy.com/soldier-life.

both *formed* by love and *informed* by love. As one scholar has put it, the virtues that express love's character and that shape the sort of persons we are have a "thirst for action," an inherent impulse to live themselves out in actions of care and concern for the neighbor. The principles that spell out further what love's obligations are toward our neighbors give direction to that thirst for action.

The expectations of the core values of loyalty and duty find their place in ethical thinking as expressions of our obligation to keep our promises. Clearly love for our neighbors would not betray their trust by breaking promises on which they depend. In the play by Thornton Wilder, *The Skin of our Teeth,* Wilder explores the human condition through the highly symbolic drama of the Antrobus family. At a critical moment in the play, Mrs. Antrobus confronts her husband with his unfaithfulness and betrayal.

> *Mrs. Antrobus:* I didn't marry you because you were perfect. I didn't even marry you because I loved you. I married you because you gave me a promise. That promise made up for your faults. And the promise I gave you made up for mine. Two imperfect people got married and it was the promise that made the marriage.

> *Mr. Antrobus:* Maggie . . . I was only nineteen.

> *Mrs. Antrobus:* And when our children were growing up, it wasn't a house that protected them; and it wasn't our love that protected them—it was that promise.[2]

Through Mrs. Antrobus, Wilder is saying more than something about marriage and adultery; he is speaking to something that is foundational for all our relationships and essential if they are to be sustainable for the mutual well-being of those involved: keeping our promises.

As love finds its ultimate expression in God's self-revelation in Christ, so also our loving God is the trustworthy and faithful God who keeps promises. Throughout the Hebrew Scripture—174 times—we are told of God's steadfast love, especially in the Psalms. Psalm 100:5 is familiar and representative: "For the Lord is good; his steadfast love endures forever, and his faithfulness to all generations." Steadfast love and faithfulness are virtues of God's promise-keeping love. They are virtues of love's commitment to the neighbor. *They provide a biblical underpinning that can readily*

---

2. Quoted in Childs, *Ethics in the Community of Promise,* 172.

enrich the warrior of faith's understanding and spiritual commitment to the virtues of loyalty and duty.

The God of the Bible is a God who makes promises. This is at the heart of the major theme of covenant. God makes a covenant promise to Abraham (Genesis 17) that his offspring will be numerous and will be given the promised land. The covenant promise is renewed with David whose throne shall be established forever (2 Sam 7:16). The people of the covenant are to be God's witnesses to the entire world, "a light to lighten the Gentiles," says the prophet Isaiah. The promised Messiah is in accord with the promise to David the Messiah will be from his lineage and will bring in the kingdom of God. This is God's ultimate promise for the future of all creation. In the Old Testament "it is the kingdom of God toward which history moves. There justice shall reign (Isaiah 11:3–5); there peace will be unbroken (Isaiah 2:2–4 and Micah 4:1–3). There Israel will at last realize her destiny to be a blessing to the entire world (Isaiah 2:3; Micah 4:2; Genesis 12:3) . . . it is God's kingdom and it will endure forever."[3]

This promise of God's future for the world weaves its way throughout the Old Testament, especially among the prophets. Against the backdrop of this long tradition of hope and expectation for the reign of God Jesus came preaching the nearness of God's kingdom. He identified his own person and work with the consummation of centuries of hope and longing for the reign of God to be manifest in its fullness.[4] Jesus' resurrection victory over sin and death became the ultimate fulfillment of God's covenant promises; in that victory the hoped for future was made present.[5] It is the future of the full realization of God's *shalom*, the Hebrew word for "peace" that is all-encompassing as it includes wholeness, unity, justice, freedom, and the triumph of life.

Ethicist Joseph Allen has made the concept of covenant promising central to his account of the Christian life and ethic. The covenant relationship that God has initiated with humanity serves as a model for the various covenants we enter into with other people in this life and the moral obligations of promise-keeping that these relationships entail. To follow God's example by living in a manner appropriate to the design of God's covenant

3. Bright, *The Kingdom of God*, 92.

4. See especially Luke 4:17–21 and Matthew 11:4–5. In both cases Jesus is presenting himself as the fulfillment of Messianic promises for God's deliverance in the prophet Isaiah.

5. See Wright, *The Challenge of Jesus*, 53, 89, 131–37, and Pannenberg, *Jesus—God and Man*, 66–88.

relationship with humankind means entrusting ourselves to one another and being faithful to the responsibilities that mutual trust involves.[6] In the present discussion we can construe the entry into military service, especially in today's volunteer armed services, as a covenant relationship in which those in service make promises to each other and entrust themselves to one another, virtually betting their lives on the keeping of the promise. The core values/virtues of loyalty and duty speak directly to the expectations of this covenant relationship.

The fulfillment of God's reign has been revealed and assured in Christ's victory, yet it is still future. We live in the "not yet" where we must walk by faith, entrusting ourselves to that promise. The way of faith and love is to seek God's *shalom* in whatever ways we can by faithfulness to our covenants in the hope of peace even in the terrible "not yet" of war. The key to the Christian ethic, wherever in life it must function, is to live in the hope and trust of God's final *shalom,* which alone makes love possible.

The Chaplain's Covenant

Chaplains not only have to provide spiritual resources to sustain warriors in their commitments to core virtues, they have to embrace those virtues in their own particular vocation. Most chaplains do not go through the same experience as other members of the military. Chaplains are commissioned differently than are most other officers, especially those who are in combat arms or are otherwise known as line officers; that is those who are in the direct line of command. There are four tracks to becoming an officer in the armed services of the United States. The first track is to attend and graduate from one of the service academies. The second track is to participate in the Reserve Officer Training Corps (ROTC) at one of many state universities participating in this program. The third track is to enlist in the military service and then attend Officer Candidate School (OCS) and upon successful completing of this course an individual is commissioned. The fourth track is to receive a direct appointment as a commissioned officer. This track is normally for those in professions needed by the military, such as physicians, other medical-related fields, lawyers, and chaplains. Unlike those who receive their commissions though one of the first three tracks, those receiving direct appointments do not attend any type of basic training other than a brief officer indoctrination course covering only the

6. Allen, *Love and Conflict,* 32–39.

rudimentary aspects of being a commissioned officer. The chaplain corps officers are the only officers whose primary obligation is to insure the first amendment rights of each individual service member are being honored. This track to commissioning and the obligation to insure the first amendment rights of every service member immediately sets the chaplain corps officer apart from other commissioned officers whose primary responsibility is to lead in combat, directly support combat operations, or provide necessary medical care in order for the service members to carry out their combat operations and contribute to the success of the missions assigned.

Chaplain corps officers are different. Chaplain corps officers are not charged with command authority or responsibility. Their task is not to lead troops, plan strategy, or carry out national command authority policy. The task of the chaplain is to insure the First Amendment rights of individuals, to care for the spiritual needs of those assigned to their care, to advise the command on religious issues, and to conduct religious services in support of the service members.

In order for a clergy person to serve as a commissioned officer all chaplain corps officers must have an ecclesiastical endorsement from a faith community recognized by the Department of Defense through the Armed Forces Chaplains Resource Board (AFCB) which is made up of the Chiefs of Chaplains and their Deputy Chiefs representing the Army, Navy, and Air Force. The US Marine Corps, the Coast Guard, and the Merchant Marine are provided chaplains through the United States Navy and thus do not have their own chaplain corps officers.

Because of the diverse make-up of the chaplain corps in the various branches of the armed services, it is difficult if not impossible to speak of them with a monolithic vocabulary. According to the National Conference on Ministry to the Armed Forces there are currently over 250 different religious faith communities recognized by the Department of Defense and most of them have some representation within the ranks of the military. While it is accurate to say that the majority of the faith communities come out of the Christian tradition not all of them do. Jewish, Islamic, Hindu, Buddhist, and other non-Christians are represented within the military and recently there has been a significant push to have the Association of Atheists and Freethinkers recognized. It is nonetheless impossible to categorize Christians except in the broadest of terms. Roman Catholic, Eastern Orthodox, and Protestant are the most obvious lines of distinction, but even here there is a broad range of Christian expression. It is possible to break the Protestant groups into evangelical, mainline, and so forth, but these categories too break under the weight of distinctiveness. *Notwithstanding this great diversity, there is a common covenantal commitment that all chaplains make that is peculiar to their vocation in ministry.*

As for Christians, *they* do not find God within themselves; we put on Christ (Rom 13:14) like a garment, which comes as a gift from outside ourselves. In the wearing of this garment and in the taking seriously the baptismal identity which it confers to us to be Christ in the world day by day, the selves are transformed.

These garments we are wearing are too large for us for we have not yet grown "to the measure of the stature of the fullness of Christ" (Eph 4:13). To the world we look like funny outsiders, which we are for we are "in the world but not of the world." The temptation is always there to throw off our ill-fitting clothes, to "go native" and fit in. This is true whether we speak of civilian clergy in parish or judicatory ministries or of clergy serving in the uniformed services of the United States. To give in and to go native is always to cede defeat.

Nowhere is this ceding of defeat more significant than in the military for here two options raise their ugly specter. First, there is the tendency to become simply one of regulars. Karl Marlantes speaks of this type of military chaplain in his book, *What It's Like to Go to War.*

> Along with food, water, mail, and ammunition came the battalion chaplain.
>
> He brought with him several bottles of Southern Comfort and some new dirty jokes. I accepted the Southern Comfort, thanked him, laughed at the jokes, and had a drink with him. Merry Christmas.
>
> Inside I was seething. I thought I'd gone a little nuts. How could I be angry with a guy who had just put his life at risk to cheer me up? And didn't the Southern Comfort feel good on that rain raked mountain top? Years later I understood. I was engaged in killing and maybe being killed. I felt responsible for the lives and death of my companions. I was struggling with a situation that approached the sacred in its terror and contact with the infinite, and he was trying to numb me to it. I needed help with the existential terror of my own death and responsibility for the death of others, enemies and friends, not Southern Comfort. I needed a spiritual guide.[7]

7. Marlantes, *What It's Like to Go to War,* 7.

When a military chaplain becomes "one of the guys" that chaplain loses the ability to serve as a spiritual guide and misses the opportunity to serve service men and women in the way that they most desperately need to be served in combat.

The second temptation is for a chaplain to become just another warrior or as is often said, "To outline the line officers." This means that a chaplain tries to be more aggressive, more of a military professional than those who are in the line of command. Chaplains who succumb to this temptation are often quick to point out defects in enlisted service members uniforms, military bearing, and physical readiness. They become preoccupied with the military aspects of their vocation and frequently pursue military education including history, tactics, and geopolitical subjects, and adopt the mannerisms, jargon, and bearing of war-fighting officers. Unfortunately this approach removes the chaplain even further from those who are already loathe to seek them out for spiritual guidance, sustenance, and support, thereby making them even more remote and less effective. *For the chaplain loyalty and duty are just as serious core virtues as for all those in service; they simply have their own particular set of obligations.*

Chapter Five

Respect and Selfless Service:
Justice and the Virtues of Love

Respect

Treat people as they should be treated. In the Soldier's Code, we pledge to "treat others with dignity and respect while expecting others to do the same." Respect is what allows us to appreciate the best in other people. Respect is trusting that all people have done their jobs and fulfilled their duty. And self-respect is a vital ingredient with the Army value of respect, which results from knowing you have put forth your best effort. The Army is one team and each of us has something to contribute.

Selfless Service

Put the welfare of the Nation, the Army and your subordinates before your own. Selfless service is larger than just one person. In serving your country, you are doing your duty loyally without thought of recognition or gain. The basic building block of selfless service is the commitment of each team member to go a little further, endure a little longer, and look a little closer to see how he or she can add to the effort.

WE HAVE ALREADY MET Reinhold Niebuhr's helpful discussion of the relationship between neighbor love, *agape*, and justice. Here we take up his idea that the two concepts can be distinguished but not separated and attempt to make their relationship to each other and to the core virtues of respect and selfless service as clear as possible.

Respect: In the Service and Beyond

Respect for autonomy is a basic general rule or general principle that gives further definition to the implications of neighbor love. Moreover, it is a basic principle found in most ethical theories and regarded by some as the foundational principal of ethics, often referred to simply as "respect for persons." When one calls for respect for "persons" one is acknowledging the other as possessing "personhood" and personhood is marked by autonomy, the dignity and responsibility of freedom. In the arena of medical practice, respect for autonomy is made clear in the insistence upon patients having the opportunity for informed consent, having the clear information they require in order to make a free, responsible choice regarding procedures that affect their well-being. The emphasis in the core virtue of respect, as stated above, does not speak directly to this dimension of autonomy. However, the notion of respect for autonomy is present in the core virtue's "respect for the dignity of others." Moreover, the expectation that they will reciprocate and the trust given that they will fulfill their duty accords to the colleagues in arms the capacity for responsible freedom in committing oneself to the common good. Autonomy as a mark of personhood means that one is one's own person but that does not mean people can do whatever they please, for personhood is relational.

Theologically, the foundation of the dignity of persons, respect for their autonomy, and the relationality that is at the core of our humanity is in the biblical doctrine of humanity's creation in the image of God.[1] The creation account in Genesis 1 tells us that humanity is created for an immediate relationship with God that distinguishes human beings from the rest of created life. This relationship we might well describe as personal. As one theologian once put it, "we are on speaking terms with God." In the command to represent God and care for the earth (Gen 1:27) we see reflected the marks of personhood: freedom and responsibility. Responsibility is inconceivable without freedom and freedom is inconceivable without responsibility.

So far so good, but the dignity and autonomy of personhood, once again, does not give leave for people to be absorbed in self-centered individualism. We are dependent beings in our very creation as *not God* but *image* of God. We are not to find the fulfillment of our existence either in

---

1. The discussion of the image of God draws on Childs, *Ethics in the Community of Promise*, 114–16.

nature or in ourselves. The intimate relationship with God that is the gift of our creation is constitutive of our being. The fall story in Genesis 3 is all about humanity's decision to succumb to the serpent's promise ("you will be like God," v.5) and step outside of that dependent relationship seeking to be fully autonomous. As the story continues, this primordial betrayal of humanity's essential relationship to the Creator inaugurates an unfolding drama of alienation from God and from one another; Adam and Eve are driven from the garden with a newfound shame, and soon Cain will kill Abel. Were it not for divine mercy and grace, ultimately revealed in the redeeming work of Jesus, the Christ, humanity would self-destruct. Instead God means to perfect us in that image through Christ's work. This is the promise of the resurrection when God's future is realized in all its fullness.[2]

The relationality of humanity's creation in the image of God is not only about relationship with God. Our relationship with one another and the whole of creation is also essential to true humanity. The well-known words of John Donne ring true: "No man is an Island, entire of itself; every man is a piece of the Continent, a part of the main . . . ." The entire story of the Bible from the primordial myth of the fall to the conclusion of the New Testament, is about humanity's struggle with its alienation from God and from each other (we should add also from the care of the earth) and the actions of God's relentless love and mercy to bring all things together in the final wholeness of his peace (*shalom*). Just as the first table of the Decalogue speaks to our relationship with God, calling forth the trust of faith and love, so the rest of the commandments spell out some of the implications of the command to love neighbor as self. Indeed, the relationship with God and each other for which humanity is created and redeemed, finds its exemplar in the relationship of the Father, Son, and Spirit, who dwell within each other in the bonds of love as one God. As the image of God we are destined for the image of the Trinity. In the meantime, in the not-yet–in-between time, during the struggle with the sins of unfaith and alienation and hostility, we seek the grace of the Spirit to grow in faith and love.

From the vantage point of faith, all this theological grounding of our innate relationality and the mutual respect it entails provides a point of

2. The discussion of the image of God in the New Testament is quite complicated. However, a few things will suffice for the present. When Christ is called "image of God" in the New Testament, it is a reference to his divinity. First Corinthians 15: 44–49 tells us that in the resurrection we will bear the image of the "heavenly man" (Jesus, the Christ). Thus, as we are perfected in the resurrection according to Christ's image, we are perfected in the image of God.

contact with the core virtue of respect as it is spelled out for military life. To be sure, military life is structured in strict ways of command and obedience, but no structure, however rigid in design, can provide success in mission if it fails to respect that which is essential to authentic humanity. This is especially critical when the people involved are being called upon to witness and participate in acts of war that could readily be called inhuman.

The core virtue of respect points to the maintenance of our humanity's essential relationality in the interdependent community of military life and work. Moreover the admonition to self-respect for the person of faith finds support in God's affirmation of our destiny in the image of God and the dignity with which God endows our humanity through that promise; the command is to love your neighbor "as yourself." Moreover, the concluding affirmation in the explanation of this core value that each one has a contribution to make gives further grounding to self-worth. It has its analogy in the theology of the church. In 1 Corinthians 12:12–31, St. Paul describes the church as the body of Christ which, like the human body, has different members having different indispensable and interconnected functions that enable the body to flourish. Having comrades whose manifold capacities work together for the common good of the mission is good news whether we are speaking of the church or the corps.

Earlier we spoke of the chaplain's responsibility to minister to all faiths as requiring respect for autonomy and resulting in justice as fairness, the fairness of equal dignity and equal treatment. Here too the cultivation of mutual respect for one's dignity as a person is essential to egalitarian justice. Only from this starting point can we move on to assert that justice demands equal opportunity, opportunity unfettered by prejudice and discrimination. And only in light of these two principles of equal dignity and opportunity can we act upon the formal principles of justice that go back to Aristotle: "to each according to their due and similar treatment for similar cases." Whether we are speaking of distributive justice (e.g., opportunity for advancement) or retributive justice, penalties for violation of law or rules or orders, the principles that flow from equal dignity reflect the demands of love in the structures of justice. And, in our not-yet world, rewards and punishments justly administered will reflect both the variety of our gifts and the reality of our failures, but in no case will it nullify the demand of neighbor love to go beyond the limits of justice to continue caring. A chaplain whom I (James Childs) know well confided to me the deep meaning she found in ministry to those imprisoned in the brig. Retributive justice had spoken but love continued unabated through the ministry of this chaplain. Others in the chaplaincy would surely have a similar testimony.

But now we must ask, "Does respect and all that we have said about it theologically, from the standpoint of the military, and in relation to justice stop with one's own or does it extend even to the enemy?" Respect for persons as an expression of neighbor love shares with that attitude and practice of neighbor love the virtue of compassion. We have already noted the compassion that Jesus displayed as our example. We should also recall Col. Franklin Eric Wester's contention that it is important for soldiers to understand themselves as not only part of a unit but also part of the human race. Internalizing that connection can go far toward understanding that even the enemy is a part of the human race and, thereby, mitigating abuses. Wester's observation correlates well with respect for persons as a keystone of justice and an expression of neighbor love that calls forth compassion.

Karl Marlantes contends that "Compassion must be elicited consciously in warfare. Our natural tendency is to think of the enemy as an animal inferior to us. This helps the warriors accomplish very ugly tasks, but it brings on unnecessary suffering if not constantly checked."[3] Like the ancient warriors who incorporated ritual in connection with their combat, Marlantes believes time must be taken outside combat for rituals that preserve our humanity. He then recounts how he punished some kids in his unit for cutting off the ears of dead enemy soldiers by making them bury their bodies. Unexpectedly the task brought tears to the eyes of these soldiers. "Why don't we bury our enemies with ceremony?" he asks.[4]

> You have heard that it was said, "You shall love your neighbor and hate your enemy." But I say to you, Love your enemies and pray for those who persecute you, so that you may be children of your Father in heaven; for he makes his sun rise on the evil and on the good, and sends rain on the righteous and on the unrighteous. For if you love those who love you, what reward do you have? Do not even the tax collectors do the same? And if you greet only your brothers and sisters, what more are you doing than others? Do not even the Gentiles do the same? Be perfect, therefore, as your heavenly Father is perfect (Matt 5: 43–48).

The Apostle Paul echoes these words of Jesus in Romans 12:14–21, where he admonishes Christians to bless those who persecute them (v. 14) and

---

3. Marlantes, *What It Is Like to God to War*, 77–78.
4. Ibid.

not to seek vengeance which belongs to God (v. 19). At the same time in Romans 13, he upholds the authority of government to bear the sword for the punishment of evildoers (v. 4). Christian warriors live in the tension reflected in Paul's Letter to the Romans. However, the fact that Paul carries forward Jesus' teaching while acknowledging the need for deadly force in a broken world should be an assurance to those that bear the tragic burdens of war, that one may still in a real sense love one's enemies, as we shall have further opportunity to observe in in the discussion of just war thinking. If armed conflict is to serve a just cause it cannot arise out of dehumanizing hatred and the lust of vengeance.

Respect: In the Service and Beyond

We have already said a good deal about the self-giving nature of *agape* love as this relates to the character of the chaplain as servant leader. This dimension of neighbor love's character obviously fits with the core value/virtue of selfless service. And it fits equally well for the warrior as it does for the chaplain. Putting the welfare of the nation, the service, and one's subordinates before one's own resonates with the love commandment of Jesus.

For officers selfless service in the spirit of *agape* is a hallmark of servant leadership and, as it happens, the key to effective leadership in the armed services as in all institutions of life. Leaders who enable their subordinates to be their best by respecting and caring about their well-being create the sort of morale that makes for an effective outfit in which leadership in various forms finds expression throughout the ranks.[5] This kind of leadership with that kind of result correlates with the previous discussion of respect and the ideal that each one within the unit is making an important contribution according to their respective abilities. Those in command who seek only their own advancement are unlikely to achieve that sort of result. What is called for is a leadership and service that does one's "duty loyally without thought of recognition or gain."

Finally, the new and different tasks the military is being called upon to undertake in today's world are proving a challenge to many officers' self-understanding of their selfless service. Martin Cook speaks of the moral basis of the military profession at the core of its selfless service. It finds

5. In the world of business Max De Pree's book *Leadership is an Art* remains a clear and helpful account of servant leadership in the world of corporate life, which can be every bit as structured as the military in some key respects.

expression in those aspirations "to serve others even at the cost of personal sacrifice, and to discipline one's mind and body so that it serves a purpose larger than oneself and the pursuit of pleasure."[6] This is the moral core of military professionalism. "It is because [officers] see themselves as engaged in defense of the values, security, and prosperity of their family and nation that their service has moral meaning."[7] However, in this post-Cold War environment this morally charged professional ethos of self-giving service is being challenged by the new strategies the military is expected to implement. These strategies include peacekeeping and peace-enforcement requiring larger numbers of civil affairs and psychological operations units. Conventional training for high-end combat traditionally at the heart of the military profession may not be the best fit for the present realities. Military professionals shaped in that tradition may wonder if the moral character of their commitment has been undermined somehow.[8] There is then a new dimension of selfless service: an adaptation to new forms of duty that involves giving up previous assumptions that grounded one's sense of professional integrity.

6. Cook, *The Moral Warrior*, 40.

7. Ibid. 74–75.

8. Ibid. 76–77.

Chapter Six

Honor and Integrity: The "Core" of the Core Values

> **Honor**
>
> Live up to Army values. The Nation's highest military award is The Medal of Honor. This award goes to Soldiers who make honor a matter of daily living—Soldiers who develop the habit of being honorable, and solidify that habit with every value choice they make. Honor is a matter of carrying out, acting, and living the values of respect, duty, loyalty, selfless service, integrity and personal courage in everything you do.
>
> **Integrity**
>
> Do what's right, legally and morally. Integrity is a quality you develop by adhering to moral principles. It requires that you do and say nothing that deceives others. As your integrity grows, so does the trust others place in you. The more choices you make based on integrity, the more this highly prized value will affect your relationships with family and friends, and, finally, the fundamental acceptance of yourself.

IN KEEPING WITH THE pattern of these chapters we have again reproduced the statement of the Army's core values, this time on honor and integrity. The concepts are virtually interchangeable as they occur in the various armed services, one emphasizing one another the other, but with similar claims that honor and/or integrity are foundational for all core values.

United States Army: Integrity

Integrity means to firmly adhere to a code of moral and ethical principles. Every Soldier must possess high personal moral standards and be honest in word and deed.

Living and speaking with integrity is very hard. You must live by your word for everything—no buts, no excuses. Having integrity and being honest in everything you say and do builds trust. For example, let's say your artillery crew accidentally damages an expensive artillery round of ammunition. This will result in an AR 15–6 investigation. Instead of telling the battery commander you damaged the round, you decide to stretch the truth and tell him the round was defective. When the battery commander discovers the truth, he will question your integrity from that moment on.

Integrity is the basis for trust and confidence that must exist among members of the Army. It is the source for great personal strength and is the foundation for organizational effectiveness. As leaders, all Soldiers are watching and looking to see that you are honest and live by your word. If you make a mistake, you should openly acknowledge it, learn from it, and move forward.

United States Air Force: Integrity

The Air Force starts with integrity because it is the essential element or the foundation on which other values are built. It's being honest with others as well as with yourself, and doing what's right at all times. Integrity remains the very bedrock of the military profession. Service members possessing integrity will always do what's right, regardless of the circumstances, even when no one is looking. They will make no compromise in being honest in small things as well as great ones.

United States Navy: Honor

"I will bear true faith and allegiance. . . . Accordingly, we will: Conduct ourselves in the highest ethical manner in all relationships with peers, superiors and subordinates; Be honest and truthful in our dealings with each other, and with those outside the Navy; Be willing to make honest recommendations and accept those of junior personnel; Encourage new ideas and deliver the bad news, even when it is unpopular; Abide by an uncompromising code of integrity, taking responsibility for our actions and keeping our word; Fulfill or exceed our legal and ethical responsibilities in our public and personal lives twenty-four hours a day. Illegal or improper behavior or even the appearance of such behavior will not be tolerated. We are accountable for our professional and personal behavior. We will be mindful of the privilege to serve our fellow Americans."

United States Marine Corps: Honor

Honor guides Marines to exemplify the ultimate in ethical and moral behavior; to never lie, cheat, or steal; to abide by an uncompromising code of integrity; respect human dignity; and respect others. The quality of maturity, dedication, trust, and dependability commit Marines to act responsibly; to be accountable for their actions; to fulfill their obligations; and to hold others accountable for their actions

United States Coast Guard: Honor

"We demonstrate uncompromising ethical conduct and moral behavior in all of our personal and organizational actions. We are loyal and accountable to the public trust."[1]

Whether stated as Integrity or as Honor, this shared core value calls members of the Armed Forces of the United States to embody, embrace, and exhibit the highest degree of moral and ethical behavior. For each of the military services being good stewards of the national trust is essential to maintaining the support of the American people. Unique among the military services of the various nations around the globe, each and every man and woman, officer and enlisted, of the armed services of the United States swears an oath of fealty not to any person but to the Constitution of the United States. It is this oath of fealty to the Constitution that forms the bedrock of the moral and ethical behavior of every service member.

Integrity or honor as a core value for the military is indeed a beginning point for the type of moral and ethical reflection that is essential to the spiritual well-being of a warrior. Through study, reflection, analysis, and synthesizing these core values warriors have an important tool that

---

1. Each of these definitions is taken from the respective Core Values Statements of the military service indicated.

can help to prevent or at least mitigate the effects of what otherwise might be a terminal wound to the soul. While it would be an absurd presumption to view the military of the United States as a Christian organization, it is nevertheless the case that much of the moral and ethical thinking with regard to the waging of war by the United States has been and continues to be deeply influenced by the just war tradition. *Jus in bello* and *Jus ad bellum* have been and remain integral parts of framing and governing the conduct of American service members in kinetic engagements with the enemy as well as guiding how the American government makes its decisions as to whether or not, and how, it is going to employ its military power as a tool in the political arsenal within geopolitical engagements.

Nonetheless the duty of military leadership to promote and preserve the honor and integrity of the service must at times face serious and disconcerting incidents that threaten the reputation and morale of the service. In 2012 at the Pentagon General James Amos, Commandant of the United States Marine Corps, gathered Marine officers, commissioned and non-commissioned, for a heartfelt presentation entitled "Who Are We and Who We Are Not?"[2] His speech was prompted by concern for the honor of the Corps in the wake of highly publicized incidents: the suicide of a corporal apparently triggered by hazing, the video of marines urinating on enemy corpses, standing in front of a Nazi SS flag. And the larger and most severe problem: female marines being subjected to rape and sexual assault by other marines, which General Amos believes is 80 percent accurate, there having been 344 cases in the year preceding his address.

In the face of these egregious actions he was at pains to remind his fellow marines what their honorable heritage is, a heritage he referred to as "almost spiritual," being careful to avoid an explicitly religious connotation. In this he echoed the admonition of a former commandant, General Mundy, who told him the he was "solely responsible for the spiritual health of the marine corps." The task is to promote and preserve the ethos of the Corps and its "special spirit" that guides choices. "Should you fail to maintain the spiritual health of the Corps," his predecessor concluded, "you will fail as commandant." Though making it clear that 99.9 percent of the marines have "kept their honor clean," to quote the marine hymn, General Amos called on the leadership, beginning with himself, to root out these problems. He called for leadership accountability in addressing violations of the ethos of the Corps, a renewed emphasis on discipline, and an all-out

2. "Commandant," *Marine Corps Times.*

effort to stop sexual assault and hazing. To this the Sergeant Major stressed that we are our brothers' and sisters' keepers; "the way we treat people absolutely does matter."

The Army's final core value, personal courage, as they define it, follows from the concerns of integrity and honor.

> **Personal courage**
>
> Face fear, danger or adversity (physical or moral). Personal courage has long been associated with our Army. With physical courage, it is a matter of enduring physical duress and at times risking personal safety. Facing moral fear or adversity may be a long, slow process of continuing forward on the right path, especially if taking those actions is not popular with others. You can build your personal courage by daily standing up for and acting upon the things that you know are honorable.

When we think about personal courage from the vantage point of the Christian ethic we immediately think of the martyrs of the faith and all the faithful, from the beginning of Christianity to the present, who, to paraphrase the Army's statement, "daily stand up for and continue to stand up for and act upon the things that they know are faithful in the sight of God." Such courage has not only been exemplified by a refusal to deny their Lord in the face of persecution but also by readiness to work for justice and just causes. The theologian and martyr Dietrich Bonhoeffer is a familiar example of courageous sacrifice in the face of great evil. As Hitler's regime was growing ever more powerful in his native Germany, Bonhoeffer was enjoying acclaim and security teaching in New York at Union Seminary. His American colleagues encouraged him to remain in the United States, where he could continue his work in safety. However, Bonhoeffer decided he must return to Germany and take up his ministry there. He was imprisoned and eventually executed shortly before the end of the war for his part in the resistance to Hitler. In reflecting on Matthew 5:10, "Blessed are those who are persecuted for righteousness sake," Bonhoeffer scolded those Christians who failed to bear witness against the injustices of the Nazis. The beatitude, he maintained, refers to persecution for all just causes—not just for witness to the Christ:

> With this beatitude Jesus thoroughly rejects the false timidity of those Christians who evade any kind of suffering for a just, good,

and true cause because they supposedly could have a clear conscience only if they were to suffer for the explicit confession of faith in Christ. . . . Jesus cares for those who suffer for a just cause even if it is not exactly for the confession of his name.[3]

The virtue of courage in military service on behalf of a just cause finds support in these words of Bonhoeffer's.

Ethicist Robin Lovin, in discussing the cardinal virtues of classical tradition, says that, "What makes courage a cardinal virtue is that we cannot act on any of the virtues for very long without it."[4] Daniel Maguire adds that, "Thomas Aquinas says that courage is the precondition of all morality and virtue. If you don't have it, your commitment to persons and the earth is specious. Courage is love ready to risk. Where there is no readiness to risk, there is no love."[5]

Personal courage in the face of adversity, an essential and governing core value or virtue of military service, finds resonance in the Christian tradition's understanding and history of courage as a virtue of love in the service of faith and justice or, in the Army's term, "of the things that you know are honorable."

---

3. Bonhoeffer, *Ethics*, 346.

4. Lovin, *Christian Ethics*, 72.

5. Maguire, *A Moral Creed for All Christians*, 105.

PART III

The Vocation of Ethical Leadership

Preamble

How are we to understand the role of the military chaplain with respect to the bedrock core value of honor/integrity, and as the embodiment of those core values? The military chaplain, by virtue of holding an ecclesiastical endorsement from a recognized religious community, is the interpreter of both the moral and ethical traditions of the religious community, and the interpreter of the moral and ethical implications of the just conduct of kinetic military operations. The chaplain helps the individual soldier to reckon with the moral ambiguities arising out of combat, and to advise the command on the overall conduct of the prosecution of the war. Therefore it is incumbent upon the chaplain to be not only well schooled in moral theology and ethics but to also be a master of the ability to reflect upon the real-world challenges and applications of those moral principles in the context of military operations within armed conflict. One of the essential skills needed by the military chaplain is that of critical thinking.

From the initial entry point into military service soldiers (here used in a generic sense to include all warriors irrespective of branch of service) receive military training intended to transform a civilian into a warrior. From the first hour in basic training throughout a military career, whether one enlistment or a full career, soldiers and officers train to fight, and to think clearly amid the chaos and fog of war. Chaplains and other professionals such as doctors and lawyers not only train as warriors but they also train as professionals. Military chaplains are required to possess a Master of Divinity degree or its equivalent, at least two years of parish experience, ordination by a faith community, and an ecclesiastical endorsement granted by a faith community recognized by the Department of Defense through the Armed Forces Chaplains Board,certifying that the individual chaplain is fully qualified to represent the faith community, to provide specific care to individuals of that faith community, and to be able to function well within the context of a broadly pluralistic and interfaith environment in order to insure the First Amendment rights of all service members and their families. This is understandably a very tall order. The Department of Defense has the responsibility to train soldiers in the art of warfare and in the skills needed by individuals in order to function effectively within the context of military service. However, there are two areas especially needed by military chaplains that can only come from the chaplain's faith community. These two special skills, if we might define them so, are the ability to *think critically* about soldiers and their work as warriors, and *spiritual intelligence* as it is currently being named.

While there is no consensus for a specific definition of critical thinking, there are generally agreed upon notions of what critical thinking is. Critical thinking is the intellectual process of gathering, organizing, evaluating, and employing information in a systematic and repeatable fashion as a guide to belief and action. Critical thinking then is a set of specific skills for gathering and evaluating information in order to act in such a way that belief is not compromised, and is an ongoing intellectual commitment to using those skills to guide one's behavior.

Critical thinking is, then, not only a mode of thinking but is also a skill that must be cultivated and developed over the course of a lifetime. For military chaplains the critical thinking skill must be informed by one's theological education and by one's spiritual formation as a priest or pastor of the faith community. The basic educational requirements of an undergraduate degree, a Master of Divinity or its equivalent, and relevant parish ministry experience are all essential elements of the development of critical thinking skills. These critical thinking skills will, of course, be profoundly challenged as they are practiced in a combat environment, whether on board combat ships at sea, among ground soldiers in active kinetic engagements, at battlefield aid stations or field hospitals, and, most recently, among those serving the remotely piloted aircraft community. The myriad of challenges posed to a military chaplain require ongoing training no less rigorous that the ongoing military training conducted daily in all line units of the military including the United States Army, the United States Navy and Marine

Corps, the United States Air Force, and the United States Coast Guard. The critical thinking skills must continually be honed if the military chaplain is going to provide effective care and counsel to warriors, and if the chaplain is going to be, in essence, protected from the potentially mortal wounds to the soul resulting from armed combat.

A military chaplain who is proficient in the skills of critical thinking must be able to employ those skills in the most hostile and chaotic of environments. Numbered among the most important of these critical thinking skills are the following:[1]

- The ability to raise and clearly and precisely state questions with regard to the nature of the conflict and its moral and ethical implications.

- The ability to gather relevant information and to interpret and assess that information to come to well reasoned solutions which have been tested against the criteria established by moral theology and ethical standards.

- The ability to think open-mindedly and independently about other systems of thought, recognizing and evaluating their assumptions, implications, and practical consequences.

- The ability to engage in effective communication with others of varying degrees of rank and positional authority to propose solutions to highly complex and ambiguous questions and problems.

Military chaplains, however strongly motivated to be keepers of moral and ethical behavior, can only achieve this goal if they know what is morally and ethically right. Military chaplains live out their vocational calling within a context that often causes the individual to confuse moral actions with vested self-interest. Even more dangerous as a pitfall to maintaining a true heading with regard to a chaplain's moral compass is the danger of

---

1. Adapted from Paul and Elder, *The Miniature Guide to Critical Thinking Concepts and Tools*. See also this definition from the American Philosophical Association: "Critical Thinking is essential as a tool of inquiry. As such, Critical Thinking is a liberating force in education and a powerful resource in one's personal and civic life. While not synonymous with good thinking, Critical Thinking is a pervasive and self-rectifying human phenomenon. The ideal critical thinker is habitually inquisitive, well-informed, trustful of reason, open-minded, flexible, fair-minded in evaluation, honest in facing personal biases, prudent in making judgments, willing to reconsider, clear about issues, orderly in complex matters, diligent in seeking relevant information, reasonable in the selection of criteria, focused in inquiry, and persistent in seeking results which are as precise as the subject and the circumstances of inquiry permit." Facione, "Critical Thinking."

falling prey to "groupthink." Irving Janis, a pioneer in the field of group-think theory described the danger of groupthink as such:

> The main principle of groupthink, which I offer in the spirit of Parkinson's Law is this: The more amiability and esprit de corps there is among the members of a policy-making ingroup, the greater the danger that independent critical thinking will be replaced by groupthink, which is likely to result in irrational and dehumanizing actions directed against outgroups.[2]

In order to guard against falling into groupthink, chaplains must have a highly developed and well-practiced understanding of their own theological grounding of what is morally right. Because of the significant institutional peer pressure of the military ethos and due to the isolating nature of military members from their civilian communities, it is essential that military chaplains train and daily practice critical thinking skills related to moral and ethical reasoning regarding mortal combat and their unique role within its conduct. Without solid grounding and constant training military chaplains are particularly vulnerable to the foibles of pseudo-morality and the increased potential for wounds to the soul which threaten to become mortal wounds to the soul, among which "compassion fatigue," discussed above, is but one presenting symptom.

To critical thinking intelligence we think it important to add the concept of "spiritual intelligence." It seems to us an appropriate expansion upon what has already been said about servant leadership. Spiritual intelligence is a concept developed recently by Cindy Wigglesworth.[3] She has built particularly upon the work of Daniel Coleman and Richard Boyatzis on what they have defined as "emotional intelligence" and its essential importance for effective leadership, including leadership in the military.[4] Wigglesworth

---

2. Janis, "Groupthink."

3. Wigglesworth," Spiritual Intelligence and Why It Matters."

4. See Boyatzis, *The Competent Manager*. Half of the public sector samples were from the ranks of the military. Dr. Boyatzis kindly responded to our inquiry regarding his work with the following comments in a July 8, 2013 email: "All of the hundreds of competency studies show that effective leaders from Chief Petty Officers to Vice Admirals, and the same in the Marines, use a distribution of emotional and social intelligence, as well as cognitive intelligence competencies. When they talked about style, it was the inspirational leaders and the developmental coaches that were effective. The quote often said to me during the interviews on board ships, at the Pentagon, and elsewhere, was that they use 'ask and inspire' NOT command and control. Actually evidence shows that effective military leaders have not used command and control for 100 years or more!"

has reframed the four clusters of emotional intelligence competencies—self-awareness, other awareness, self-management, relationship skills—in spiritual but nonsectarian terms. In her formulation there is a vertical component grounded in "something sacred, divine, timeless" and a horizontal component expressed in "being of service to our fellow humans and to the planet at large." The vertical component includes, among others, competencies of awareness of one's own world view and awareness of life's purpose, commitment to spiritual growth, living one's purpose and values, and seeking guidance from a "Higher Power." The horizontal component includes, among others, competencies of awareness of the interconnectedness of all life, awareness of the world views of others, the capacity to be a wise and effective spiritual mentor and a wise and effective change agent who makes compassionate and wise decisions. In her research, leaders who possess these competencies in significant measure are described as, "loving, kind, forgiving, peaceful, courageous, honest, generous, persistent, faithful, wise, and inspiring."

Some leaders may be more gifted for the development of spiritual intelligence competencies by the fortunes of their personal formation. However, awareness of the importance of spiritual intelligence and a disciplined approach to nurturing its competencies and traits is an obligation of leaders in general and chaplains in particular. The intelligence competency of critical thinking is essential to all ethical discourse and decisions. However, because the ethical approach we are commending is theologically grounded and spiritually energized, emphasis upon spiritual intelligence seems totally appropriate. Moreover, it is not hard to see that the traits of spiritual intelligence as Wigglesworth enumerates them correlate nicely with what we have seen are the characteristics of servant leadership driven by *agape* and nurtured in the theology of the cross.

Chapter Seven

A Case Study in Ethical Theory

WE HAVE BEEN LOOKING at ethics from the standpoint of theologically grounded Christian principles, an appropriate spirituality, and the exercise of critical thinking amidst the terrible ambiguities of war. However, since much of the literature and instruction in military ethics operates out of traditional theories of moral philosophy, it will be helpful to see an example of such approaches at work. In this way we can see the points of contact with our version of Christian ethics but also the distinctive characteristics of a faith-based approach.

On July 19, 2010 Canadian soldier Captain Robert Semrau was convicted by a military court martial for killing a wounded Taliban fighter in Afghanistan, which was characterized in the media as a battlefield mercy killing. Dr. Peter Bradley, a retired Lieutenant-Colonel in the Canadian army who teaches psychology and ethics at the Royal Military College of Canada, has examined this case. He noted that Captain Semrau had supporters as well as detractors. Moreover, the jury did not convict him of second degree murder or attempted murder or even negligent performance of military duty but of the lesser charge of disgraceful conduct. The existence of conflicting views and the unexpected decision of the jury made for an ambiguous outcome. For Col. Bradley this outcome raised questions for the sort of ethical guidance soldiers require. Bradley therefore developed a hypothetical case of mercy killing similar to the Semrau case and examined it from the standpoint of three different decision-making models currently taught in Canadian Forces ethics courses.[1] The models used are each versions of standard models used in moral philosophy.

1. The narrative that follows is drawn from Bradley's article, "Is Battlefield Mercy

The case imagines a patrol that encounters a wounded enemy soldier who appears to be dying. There are no medical resources available to treat him and no means of evacuation to a medical facility. The patrol is not in contact with the enemy and there appears to be no immediate threat.

Bradley first looks at the case from the perspective of consequences. This is the sort of teleological reasoning associated with the utilitarianism of Jeremy Bentham and John Stuart Mill. In this approach the right choice is that which brings the greatest good and/or the least harm for the most people affected by the decision. Bradley sets down the options the patrol has and the consequences of each for those affected. Which will lead to the greatest good or the least harm? The *first choice* is to provide what medical care is possible and stay with the wounded fighter till evacuation is possible. The *second option* is to provide medical care to the extent possible and take the wounded fighter along with the patrol, either so it can complete its mission or move the casualty to a safer place. The *third option* Bradley suggests is to give the medical care possible and leave the man to fend for himself. The *fourth and final option* is to kill the wounded fighter and thereby hasten his death. This is presumably the so-called "mercy killing" option.

After detailed analysis from this consequentialist perspective, Bradley concludes that the first option will result in the greatest good and the least harm for all concerned. The mercy killing option may result in the least suffering for the wounded man but assessing the degree of suffering prevented may be beyond the ability of the forces. Negative consequences of taking a life in contravention of various laws and codes could alone be significant. If, on the other hand, the nature of the mission involved the saving of lives, the second option might be justified. One can begin to see that decisions based on possible consequences can involve some real uncertainties and can also verge on the dangers of "the ends justify the means" reasoning.

Bradley next moves to consider the case from a deontological or principle-based approach associated historically with the work of Immanuel Kant. Bradley applies two tests from the obligations entailed in Kant's "categorical imperative." First, we should never treat persons as a means to an end but always as ends in themselves, thereby protecting the dignity of all. The second test is that of "universalizability": would everyone in a similar situation be morally justified in taking the action contemplated? If the actions taken pass these two tests, they may be considered morally justified. Bradley believes that option 1 passes both tests and that option 2 would

Killing Morally Justifiable?"

pass both tests as long as moving the causality is for his security rather than in the interests of the patrol's ability to carry on with their other duties.

Finally Bradley looks at the case from the vantage point of virtue ethics, which he associates historically with Aristotle. Bradley also sees this approach as aligned with the values or virtues the military espouses. Though he writes from the Canadian military perspective these virtues/values are basically the same as those we have looked at representing the United States services in Part II. The question here is whether or not an action is "virtuous," consistent with the virtues one associates with the moral life. Bradley believes that this approach should be used in concert with one of the other two just discussed. In this way, we would say, he is linking the ethics of "being" (the sorts of persons we are: virtue) with the ethics of "doing" (how we decide the right action, by consequences or principles), which we would want to affirm as a more complete approach to a vision of the ethical enterprise. Once again and not surprisingly Bradley sees option 1 as consistent with military virtues of loyalty, duty, and obedience, to name three. However, though consistent with the virtues or ideals named as the military understands their implications, the action taken may not be motivated by true concern for the victim. If instead it is a matter of just not wanting to get caught doing something wrong, then it may be considered less moral. (In fact, fear of violating a code or law places this response outside virtue ethics and in a more deontological mode of reasoning.) Similarly, option 2 may be morally justifiable by these criteria as long as the motives are in line with the virtues displayed. Again options 3 and 4 are rejected as in the two other approaches.

In the final analysis, we would argue that the nature of one's motives is appropriate in all approaches for a full-orbed appreciation of the moral life, even if the method employed does not require consideration of motive in reaching a decision.

As we have seen, in Bradley's analysis of the case the results are basically the same whether one uses one or the other of the three methods he describes. This is not an unusual result in the application of different theories of moral philosophy. However, it does to some degree obscure the fact that these three theories have some significant differences that in other cases may lead to markedly different conclusions concerning our obligations. A faith-based ethic may also arrive at similar conclusions in Bradley's case study. Certainly faith-based ethics will enter upon decision-making with a clear sense of *a priori* obligations reminiscent of Kant's categorical imperative but rooted in an understanding of divine will. Faith-based ethics will also be concerned about consequences as in Bradley's first approach even if this utilitarian calculus is not normative. And, it goes without saying that virtue and motive could hardly be out of consideration. From our Christian perspective this should be clear from what has already been said about *agape* as, more than an ethical directive, a way of being.

Faith-based ethics rest upon foundational claims about God and reality. They are neither simply the product of reasoning nor the offshoot of cultural traditions, despite the role both reason and culture play here as in all moral systems. The "why" of a given obligation or virtue is grounded in theological convictions concerning divine will in the creation and redemption of all things. The "way" of the moral life is driven by the grace of God's empowering love, which provides motive, capacity, and embodied example. Helmut Thielicke has put the distinction between Christian ethics and philosophical ethics in a helpful way. What distinguishes the two approaches, he says, is that they have different starting points. Philosophical ethics, as we have seen in Bradley's case, starts with the *task*; the task of determining and doing the right thing in the given situation. Christian ethics has the same task but it begins with the *gift*, the gift of the grace of God in Christ for the task ahead. (In the original German "task" is *Aufgabe* and "gift" is *Gabe*, a memorable bit of wordplay.) From the standpoint of philosophical ethics the fulfillment of the task is a matter of personal moral achievement. From the faith-based perspective it is God's grace at work in and with the person, in which divine companionship is also a source of strength and comfort in the face of terrible moral struggles.[2]

Chaplains may not be charged with the duty of providing ethics training and ethics training for the general population in the military will likely not be faith based. Nonetheless, the development of a faith-based approach to ethical discernment and decision is an integral part of the chaplain's pastoral vocation. It involves sustaining the integrity of the values of military life we have already reviewed and it helps warriors keep faith and duty together in the face of terrible choices and troubled consciences. Thus, the ethical vocation of the chaplain is more than simply inculcating some principles or a decision-making method. It is a full-orbed ministry to the whole person. Nowhere is the need for such a ministry more poignantly illustrated than in confronting the phenomenon that has come to be known as "moral injury." The discussion of moral injury will lead us back to further

2. Thielicke, *Theological Ethics*, 51–52.

thoughts about the viability of just war thinking as essential to the pursuit of military ethics in any meaningful way. First this transition:

From the Personal History of Wollom Jensen

I begin my discussion of moral injury with a personal narrative. My own experience as a young enlisted soldier, a draftee in South Vietnam, is offered as a means of sharing my own personal account of suffering a moral injury.

It has been forty-six years since I returned home following a tour of duty with the 25th Infantry Division in South Vietnam. It seems like only yesterday and yet it is buried in the far distant past of my own biography. I returned to my home in North Dakota on March 21, 1969 after having spent thirteen months in a combat zone. I returned as I had left, alone, as that was the way the US Army deployed soldiers, not as units but as individuals. I was met at the airport in Grand Forks not with parades or family, but by my best friend who was considerate enough to have included a case of beer in the trunk of his car for our one-hour drive from the airport to my hometown. My first week-end back I decided to attend church. I went to the parish I had grown up in. With twelve years perfect attendance in Sunday school, confirmation classes over a two-year period, singing first in the Cherub Choir and then the adult choir, performing trumpet solos and accompaniments for the Easter Sunrise Services, participation in the youth group, Summer Bible camp weeks, and vacation church school, I had been deeply engaged and was looking forward to being back in the fold.

While I was in Vietnam I had found my way back to my faith. It was not really back to my faith for I had never really left that. I, not unlike so many others of my age, had simply drifted away from the organized structure of the church as I had come to understand it. However, while I was in Vietnam I had returned. It was not some sort of foxhole conversion for me. My return to church was something of an epiphany or, as I learned much later in my life from this description given by a Navy Master Chief Petty Officer, a "BFO"—a Blinding Flash of the Obvious. I was not seeing something that had never been there before but, rather, an opening to what had been so obvious that I had never seen it before. I imagine that it was something like a person who day after day enters a familiar room in the house and one day notices a picture, a photograph, or knick-knack and exclaims, "When did we get that?" Only to be told, "It's been there since last Christmas. I just moved it to where it is now." You know, it's one of those things that blends into the background of our lives and has become so familiar that we no longer see it. It happened like that.

About eight months into my thirteen-month tour in Vietnam I had been spending quite a bit of time in the field in support of various infantry and artillery units helping to provide communications for their operations against NVA and Viet-Cong units in Tay Ninh Province. We were ordered to accompany the artillery battery back to the 25th Division Headquarters base at Cu Chi. It was good news because it meant real food, hot showers, clean uniforms, haircuts, a chilled beer, and some respite from the grueling routine of combat operations. Back in the main base camp I began to feel somewhat human again. I went to the Post Exchange (PX) to get my hair cut and just happened to see an announcement posted on the bulletin board that there was going to be a Lutheran worship service held at a small chapel in the area of the division engineer battalion. I cannot to this day tell you what compelled me to want to attend that service but I decided to give it a go. Sunday morning came. I began my walk to the chapel and realized that I would have to walk across the grounds of the 12th MEDEVAC hospital. As I was making my way I heard a voice yell, "Hey, Specialist, can you give me a hand?" It was a soldier standing next to an ambulance. "Sure, what do you need?" I replied. It turned out that he was from Graves Registration and was in the process of taking GIs from the hospital to the Graves Registration building as the first leg of their final trip home. It didn't take long to help him complete his task but when we were finished I didn't much feel like going to church. I returned to my hootch and waited for the NCO club to open so I could self-medicate my sick feelings away. While drugs such as marijuana and heroin were not difficult to find, I was never interested in using them but found much comfort and solace in "Bam di Bam," a local Vietnamese brew and, especially an American beer when they were available. The following week was fairly typical for the main base camp. Once or twice each day we could expect to receive incoming 122mm rockets or mortars and they would hit and explode somewhere within the division base camp perimeter. By this time in my tour I had become used to these events and rarely gave them much thought. After all, it was not the rockets, mortars, or bullets that you could hear that would hurt you. It was the one you didn't hear that would kill you, so as long as one's hearing was intact. "Sen Loi" (So be it). Throughout the week I was surprised that my thoughts kept returning to church. I was feeling an inexplicable urge to go to church though I tried hard to dispel it. Nevertheless, I was unable to shake the urge and Sunday morning I found myself walking to the Division Engineer Battalion on my way to a Lutheran worship service.

Once I arrived at the canvas and pole mess tent that served as the chapel I found a wooden folding chair toward the rear and took a seat. There was something vaguely familiar as several others came in and took seats as well. The chaplain assistant came to the altar, finished the set-up, and then lit the two candles on either side of the altar. For a brief moment I was carried home and thought about the many times I had served as an acolyte in my home congregation. The chaplain came to the front of the altar wearing his jungle fatigues and a stole draped around his neck. He introduced himself though his name now escapes me. I do remember that he was originally from Valley City, North Dakota, my home state and a place that I knew well since my high school basketball coach was also from there and had graduated from what was then known as Valley City State Teachers College. Following the first hymn, which was familiar to me, I settled in to the liturgy. It was all familiar to me, and for the very first time in a long while I knew what was going to happen next. I knew the words to all of the responses without having to refer to the hymnal. The readings, hymns, collects, creed, and Great Thanksgiving, were all familiar to me and I was drawn away from the chaos of what had been happening to and around me for the last several months. When the service was over I lingered around for some coffee and conversation with other soldiers and greeted the chaplain, who was soon off to conduct a field service at a fire support base called the Dau Tiiang Rubber Plantation north of us near the city of Tay Ninh. That was it! No great, earth-moving emotional experience. No deeply felt conversion experience, no tears, no waving of hands or voices. It was simply an experience of the familiar, the predictable, and the safe. It felt as though I had spent a little time at home.

My original DEROS (date eligible for return from overseas) was February 20, 1969. At the time the US Army was granting early separation for draftees who were returning from Vietnam with six months or less of obligated active service remaining. Had I gone home on my DEROS date I would have had to spend about seven months at an Army post located somewhere in the United States. That was not an option I wanted to exercise. Consequently, I voluntarily extended my overseas time by one additional month. The day following my original departure we experienced a significant ground attack and several of the guard bunkers which surrounded the main base camp at Cu Chi were overrun by Viet Cong forces, several aircraft were destroyed on the ground, and there were VC throwing satchel charges into hootches and bunkers in many places around the base camp. I was sent with many of my comrades as a rapid response force to help destroy and drive out the VC who were then occupying bunkers that they had taken during the night. 122mm Russian-made rockets were falling in aimless patterns and mortars were falling throughout the 25th Division's main base camp. As daylight broke and the heaviest of the fighting subsided the challenge of securing the base remained. I was an NCO at the time and had been issued a side arm, a .45 caliber pistol, so the company commander volunteered me to take my .45 and a flashlight and search all of the bunkers in our company area to make certain there were no VC in them lying in wait for one or more of us to enter. I was twenty years old, angry, invincible, and deeply stoic. I asked myself what I had been thinking when I extended and cursed myself for the foolishness of that decision. There was a common expression among the troops who were no longer newbies in the country: "Fuck it. It doesn't mean a thing, so march on." I took the flashlight, un-holstered my .45, cocked it, and entered the first of a dozen bunkers alone.

Three weeks later I was back in "the world" and once again on my way to church. As I walked from my car to the steps in front of the church my mind was all over the place. I thought of the many occasions I had walked up these steps with my Dad. I thought of people I knew, friends I had made, events that had occurred in this church. In a small town of 1,500 people there were not many people I did not know, especially in the congregation. There were five of us from that small town who were in Vietnam around the same time frame. One had returned in a flag-draped casket, one more would be coming home in a casket, two would return alive, as I had, and there I was, back and about to go to church. I knew that nearly everyone that Sunday morning knew who I was and that I had just returned from Vietnam. My short military haircut and the tropical suntan were dead giveaways as to who I was and where I had been. It was strange to sit in what was a familiar setting surrounded by familiar faces and yet feeling so unfamiliar. While I saw people looking at me with recognition in their eyes, no one spoke to me. I began to feel anxious and I kept looking around, not sure what I was hoping or expecting to see. My concentration began to diminish and I had a remote sense of wanting to be somewhere else. When the pastor began his sermon I was really uncomfortable and wishing that the service was over. What I heard from the pulpit was one of the most vehement anti-war sermons I have ever heard. Sweat broke out on my forehead and my mouth went dry. I was the only Vietnam veteran present that Sunday morning and I was certain that the sermon was directed at me. Anger filled me and I was raging inside feeling terrifyingly alone. I wasn't home, I wasn't among friends, I was surrounded by strangers who I was certain were viewing me as an unwanted presence. By the time the sermon was finished, I was a wreck. I was in the midst of an oncoming panic attack and I just wanted out of that place. As the service concluded I fled. I couldn't get out and away quickly enough. No coffee, no conversation, no welcome home, no good to see you. I left that day and now over forty years later, I still have never returned to that place, nor do I have any desire to.

What I have come to realize now I didn't know then. Men and women returning from a tour of duty in a combat zone are all wounded. Some wounds are worse and more serious than others. Many wounds are visible; some are not. Some wounds are mortal while others are survivable. Some wounds heal quickly while other wounds never really heal but just ache throughout a veteran's lifetime, perhaps much the way Jacob's hip ached for the rest of his life.

During my tour of duty in Vietnam I had seen, heard, smelled, tasted, and done many things no human being should ever have to see, hear, smell, taste, or do. I had seen people killing and being killed or injured. I had heard the sounds of outgoing and incoming rounds, artillery and bombs. I had heard the cries of the wounded and dying, and I had heard the curses of both the killers and the killed. I smelled the stench of rotting bodies and burning shit. I had tasted the thick odor of death in the air. I had fired my weapon wildly and I had taken a cold aim with a perfect sight picture at the end of my M-16 and followed the round to its impact point and watched a man fall. I had experienced things that so conflicted with my midwestern, Lutheran upbringing and piety that now over forty-five years later I still have occasional bad dreams about them. While I have no visible wounds or scars to show for my combat experience, I bear the scars of moral injury. I also carry the scars shown only on X-rays of the multiple myeloma that continues to threaten me as a presumed result of the Agent Orange I was exposed to as a soldier in Vietnam. None of us, not a single person who goes to war comes home uninjured. Not a single one!

What I'm talking about here is a relatively new term, "moral injury." This term is finding currency within the mental health profession, especially among those who are working with veterans. "Moral injury" is used to describe the injury—I hesitate to use "psychological"—suffered by warriors whose actions in combat contradict their ethical values and moral beliefs. The norm most of us have been taught is that there are certain behaviors that are simply unacceptable within families and society in general. We spend years raising our *children to adhere to these values; most often underscored within a religious context that defines actions and behaviors that are an offense to God as sin. I was raised within that context as I described earlier. There is a religious legalism that is drawn upon to aid parents in the raising of "good boys and girls." My grandmother was particularly adept at using this technique. She was a Danish Lutheran Pietist. Within her religious and theological framework, she believed that many actions and behaviors were offensive to God and therefore had to be avoided at all times. Modesty, sobriety, temperance, and suffering in silence were among the virtues she embraced. I often describe her as a woman sitting at her small dining room table wringing her hands, worried that somewhere someone was having a good time and she couldn't stand it. On the other hand, she was a Sunday school teacher of many, many years' duration. She was circumspect in her language and only once in my life did I hear her utter an oath stronger than "blame," which she used to underscore her strong feelings such as when I accidently turned the radio on too a high volume and she came scampering into the room shouting, "Turn that blame thing down!" She lived her life as she taught it and she will always have a very special place in my heart. However, her ethical values and moral beliefs reinforced by my religious upbringing were problematic for me when I was drafted into the US Army in the summer of 1967. This inner conflict became especially acute as I struggled to make sense of what I was experiencing and later had experienced as a combat support soldier in South Vietnam. This part of my warrior experience has been going on inside of me for over forty years now.*

Moral injury is not a Diagnostic and Statistical Manual-*recognized mental disorder or condition. Moral injury does not respond to common therapeutic protocols and is not a medical condition. Within those who have received moral injuries there is experienced a profound sense of alienation and abject shame. The good news is that these feelings are entirely appropriate and are indicators that the individual has a moral compass that has been compromised and is in need of recalibrating. Moral injury results not only from the actions taken by an individual, but it results also from what the individual witnesses in an area of kinetic combat operations.*

Although I, personally, never had to shoot at a woman or child, I did witness such an event. While driving in a convoy from Cu Chi to the base camp located near Tay Ninh City we were stopped by Military Police who were providing security and escort to the convoy. The potential for an ambush of any convoy was always a very serious and ever-present concern. The MPs were checking out a fruit stand that was located on the side of the road we were following. After several minutes a flurry of activity erupted. There were suddenly shouts and yelling, people scattering in all directions followed by a burst of automatic weapons fire from the jeep mounted M-60 machine gun manned by an MP. Very quickly we were ordered to move out and our two-and-a-half-ton trucks roared into action. As our column moved onward we passed the spot where Vietnamese civilians, some RVN (Republic of Vietnam) troops, and several MPs from the 25th Division were gathered around a small body located several yards away from the fruit stand. As we passed by, I recognized that the small body was that of a child who had just been killed by the MP still standing at the ready and prepared to fire again if necessary. I learned a short while later that the shout, yelling, and flurry of activity had been in response to the child suddenly holding a hand grenade. The child was trying to pull the pin of the grenade thus arming it in preparation for his throwing it into the back of one of our convoy trucks as we slowly passed by the fruit stand. I will never forget the looks of the horror-stricken civilians nor the sickening sight of that bloodied child lying in the dirt on the side of the road. It was much later that I learned that the child had been only eleven years old. What I witnessed that day did not match up with the ethical principles or moral values I had been taught by people such as my grandmother. The event caused a fugue within me, a cognitive dissonance that put me in a state of conflict between what I believed about moral behavior and what had witnessed as a necessity of war. Who was right? Who was wrong? Was it the MP who was doing his best to protect the lives of those with whom he served and who were depending upon him to do his job and keep them safe? Was it the child who had somehow been convinced that it was a heroic act to throw a hand grenade into a truck filled with American soldiers? Following thirteen months of exposure to and participation in what was then called "ground operations" against a hostile and determined enemy, I was filled with anger, shame, guilt, and disgust. But those feelings did not surface until after I had left Vietnam and returned home. At the time of the incident involving the death of a child, I, like most of those with whom I served, had adapted to the environment. Following a brief time of disgust at what I had seen along the road to Tay Ninh I fell back upon the attitude expressed in the slogan, "It doesn't mean anything, fuck it! March on!"

I believe now that my urge, a sense of calling, to attend that Lutheran worship service came when it did because I was on the downward side of my tour in Vietnam. Although I still had a couple of months remaining "in country" I was beginning to think of going home. This is a dangerous time *for soldiers because you develop what's known as a "short-timer's" attitude and whether you realize it or not you've begun the process of returning to "the world"—home, civilization, safety, comfort, family, and friends. What I knew instinctively but could never have articulated was that I returned to the church to find predictability, safety, order over chaos, and a sense of sanity in what I had come to understand as the insanity that attends to going to war. I had become as Jonathan Shay would come to describe a warrior, Achilles in Vietnam, and in very real sense my character had become undone. I can remember the moment when that undoing occurred.*

I had been in Vietnam for less than two months. Following a brief period that included orientation, acclimatization, and mortar and rocket attacks every hour around the clock, I was sent into the field to support an artillery battery with communications. Now nearly two months into my tour, I was jumpy, hyper-reactive, scared, and tired. I was having difficulty sleeping and didn't have much of an appetite, especially for the C-rations we were eating in the field. We got word that we were all returning to the main division base camp at Cu Chi and we loaded our gear into a C47 Chinook helicopter and flew back to Cu Chi. That evening I was standing with a group of soldiers from my platoon chatting and drinking a beer as the sun was about to set. I was sitting atop a row of sandbags that surrounded our hootch. Suddenly, one of the guys, a sergeant name Glenn Smith, shouted, "Look out!" and as everyone scattered I dove off of the sandbags and landed sprawling in the dirt, my beer spilling all over me. As I scrambled to my feet to run to the nearest bunker for safety from what I expected to be shrapnel, I heard gales of laughter. I looked around to see all my friends, especially "Smitty," doubled over in laughter at my reaction. I was humiliated, and angry at having been made such a fool of. However, I later came to realize that that experience was the moment I became insane. My world was insane, unpredictable, deadly, grotesque, and unlike anything I could ever have imagined. I decided that the only response to an insane situation from which I had no ability to extricate myself was to become insane myself. "It doesn't mean anything! Fuck it! March on!" I believe that this was a significant step in the course of my moral injury. The adaptation of a sane young man to an insane environment is to go insane. It sounds like something out of Joseph Heller's novel Catch 22. *The catch, of course, comes from the title. The expression really didn't come into common usage until Heller's novel was made into a movie in 1970. The catch is that a bomber pilot is considered to be insane if he continues to fly combat bombing missions without asking to be relieved from that duty. If the pilot doesn't ask* to be relieved and deemed insane, he is eligible to be relieved from that duty. However, if the pilot does ask to be relieved, he is considered to be sane and therefore must keep flying the bombing missions. While I was not yet familiar with Heller's novel nor had the movie yet been released, that is where I found myself. The world around me was insane. People were doing things to one another that are absolutely insane any place other than combat. Since I thought that I was sane, and had no way to extricate myself from the insane situation, in order to preserve my sanity, I opted to become insane. That's really what the expression, "It doesn't mean anything. Fuck it. March on!" actually means. The cognitive dissonance becomes too great and one sustains a moral injury or as some would say, a soul wound. I have had the opportunity to talk with many wounded warriors from both Iraq wars and from having been down range in Afghanistan. When we are able to talk with one another as comrades in arms, which usually takes a little time, I hear them giving voice to a similar experience and conclusion. The challenge then becomes one of finding one's way back from the insanity of war to the sanity of a civilized world. Can there be any wonder why so many veterans feel so alienated when they finally return home?

The process of returning to civilian life for combat veterans is no easy task. The adoption of the insanity of which I just spoke is a combat survival behavior for warriors. It is a means of protecting the soul or deep character that most individuals seek to keep intact. The behaviors are strategies to keep one morally and physically intact in an environment where other people are actively trying to kill you. While these behaviors might well be described as adaptive in a combat zone, many of them are hardly acceptable in a civilian environment. The question then becomes, "How do I re-adapt upon my return home. How do I undo the insanity of the catch 22 of war?"

In my case I was drawn back to the Lutheran congregation in which I had grown up. I could not have articulated that at the time; in fact it has taken me most of the last forty-plus years since my return to do that. When I went to church on my first Sunday home, I was looking for what I thought I had found in that chapel in Vietnam. I was looking for a safe space. I needed a place where I could speak my personal narrative. Indeed, I desperately needed not only to tell my narrative, but also to be assisted in forming that narrative. I needed to have people who would listen to me, encourage me, and help put words to the narrative. I needed people who would not be judgmental but also people who would not be shocked, revolted, or disgusted by it. I also sought a sacred space. I was searching for a place in which I could confess my fear, my *guilt, my shame, and be forgiven and reconciled back into the life I felt I had lost. That sacred space I sought was not to be found in that church. Looking and longing for a safe and sacred space I had gone to the one place I was certain I could find it. My disappointment that it was neither only added to my guilt, shame, alienation, and anger. Today, I am and remain a Christian not because of the church but in spite of the church. Having been an ordained clergyperson of that church has not changed my feelings for the church but it has provided me a way to repay a debt of gratitude. I ultimately answered what I believed to be a call to the ordained ministry as a way to give thanks for the gift I had been given during the worship service conducted by an Army chaplain whose name I cannot even recall.*

Chapter Eight

Moral Injury

OF THE MANY QUESTIONS arising from a warrior's participation in armed conflict one of the most common arises from seeing humanity at its absolute worst. "What happened to the good? Where did it go?" The question takes many different forms but the essence is universal. How can human beings inflict the type of carnage and destruction upon one another that warfare demands?

There is no doubt that war in the twenty-first century is unlike war in any previous century. To be sure there are similarities in the basic nature of warfare but the forms, venues, and means have evolved beyond the levels of our moral and philosophical reasoning and understanding.

Warfare in American history has always been evolutionary, especially from the standpoint of technology. Perhaps no war has shown the tragic reality of technology exceeding both military tactics and strategy more clearly than World War I. The advent of the machine gun made Napoleonic Squares and cavalry charges obsolete and resulted in what can only be described as the mass slaughter of millions of young men on the European fields of battle. However, the armies continued to collide on specific geographic spaces known as the battlefield. In fact, those battle spaces often lent their names to the battles themselves up to and through the Vietnam War. Names such as Bunker Hill, Cowpens, and Yorktown; Gettysburg, Manassas, and Vicksburg; Belleau Wood, the Somme, and the Meuse-Argon; Normandy, Sicily, Guadalcanal, and Iwo Jima; Inchon and Chosen Reservoir; Khe San, Ira Drang Valley, and Hue City help to define engagements in which opposing armies met en masse upon the fields of battle.

These battles involved significant movements of troops and engagements lasting from days to several weeks in duration, followed by relatively long periods in which little or no kinetic action occurred. Ante–twenty-first-century warfare could be described as having armies that were clearly identified as combatants, where war was waged largely on open battlefields with relatively well-defined front lines, and engagements were typically brief with lengthy periods of relative calm wedged in between them during which troops could replenish, rest, and regroup. This pattern is no longer descriptive of twenty-first-century warfare. The latter few years of the twentieth century saw the advent of terrorist bombings in 1993 by an attack on the World Trade Towers in New York City followed in 1998 with attacks on the US Embassies in Kenya and Tanzania. The second attack upon the World Trade Center in 2001 moved the whole world into twenty-first-century warfare in which the phrase "Shock and Awe" became part of the common vocabulary.

Speed, increased lethality, network-centric platforms, the loss of noncombatant exclusions, urban settings, and remotely piloted vehicles have become the standard for a new way of waging war. There are no longer clearly discernible front lines, no rear echelons, and what is now twelve years of war in which kinetic engagement has been near constant has become the new face of war.

Broken bodies and broken lives manifest the damage in increased incidents of post-traumatic stress, and suicides occurring among active soldiers and veterans in near battalion numbers each month, not to mention the spouses and other family members of service men and women, are all too common. Sexual assaults on both women and men by green on green, and moral failures of senior officers, have increased at a disturbing rate.

Beyond the physical and psychological wounds experienced by our warriors there has arisen a new class of injuries called "spiritual, soul, or moral." While there are many different definitions of moral injuries the following is taken from the US Department of Veterans Affairs and aptly describes the essence of a moral injury.

> Like psychological trauma, moral injury is a construct that describes extreme and unprecedented life experience including the harmful aftermath of exposure to such events. Events are considered morally injurious if they "transgress deeply held moral beliefs and expectations" (1). Thus, the key precondition for moral injury is an act of transgression, which shatters moral and ethical expectations that are rooted in religious or spiritual beliefs, or

culture-based, organizational, and group-based rules about fairness, the value of life, and so forth.[1]

Rita Nakashima Brock and Gabriella Lettini in their book on moral injury speak of those who have suffered such injury as feeling "they no longer live in a reliable, meaningful world and can no longer be regarded as decent human beings."[2]

Jonathan Shay says that moral injury is the persistence of adaptive behaviors to survive in a combat situation that cause a warrior to have complications in the process of readapting to a civilian environment. Moral injury to the warrior is not simply the result of experiencing the awful things that warriors are exposed to in combat. Moral injury according to Dr. Shay is the result of three parts, each of which must be present in order for a moral injury to occur. First, there must be a betrayal of what is morally correct. Second, someone who is in a legitimate position of authority must commit the betrayal of what is morally correct. Third, the betrayal must occur in a high-stakes situation.[3]

Moral injury is often not readily apparent either to the injured or to others. Not unlike post-traumatic stress or traumatic brain injury the symptoms of moral injury do not just suddenly and dramatically appear. It is more like they just emerge, coming out of the murky mist of one's inner core. Shay's three-part definition is an important contribution but a broader statement seems preferable: moral injuries are wounds from having done something, or failed to stop something, that violates a person's moral code. By this definition moral injuries are not the same as PTS with nightmares and flashbacks along with other symptoms. Moral injuries torture the soul of an individual. Moral injuries plague the conscience and are manifest by a sense of deep shame, guilt, and rage. Retired Col. Elspeth Ritchie, a former psychiatry consultant to the Army Surgeon General, asserts that "The concept of moral injury is an existentialist one. You may not have actually done something wrong by the law of war, but by your own humanity you feel that it's wrong."[4]

Col. Ritchie's observations can be illustrated by a recently published interview with a veteran of the war in Iraq who served as an Army nurse. In the wake of a bombing he took charge of those who had little chance

1. National Center for PTSD, "PTSD."

2. Brock and Lettini, *Soul Repair*, xv.

3. Shay, "Casualties."

4. Quoted in Jelinek, "Some Casualties are 'Wounded Souls,'" A22.

of survival. Among them was a little girl of perhaps six years old whose chest was blown apart. He recounts that he could not let her suffer and so he injected dose after dose of painkillers into her IV. She died then and he is sure that he killed her. Even though subsequent medical evaluation and toxicology reports showed that she died of her injuries, not his injection of pain medication, he still blames himself for her death. Now he seeks therapy with other "souls in anguish," including an Army staff sergeant who was unable to aid a comrade whose legs were severed in an explosion in Afghanistan, a Marine Iraq vet whose junior comrade was killed after he had persuaded him to switch posts, and a Navy man who beat an Iraqi civilian in anger. [5]

The notion of moral injury does not necessarily include the loss or taking of human life. Consider the following anecdote taken from WBUR 90.9, Boston's NPR station, entitled "Moral Injury: When Soldiers Betray Their Sense of Right and Wrong."

> "Tom" is an Army Veteran who deployed twice to Iraq. He lives in the suburbs of Boston and asked that we not use his real name.
>
> Tom tells a story of moral injury where nobody dies. Still, it gets at another way of defining moral injury, one in which you stand in for the person of legitimate authority, betraying your own sense of right and wrong.
>
> "With the dogs I always laugh, because people could not possibly understand. I love dogs. I grew up with dogs. But in Iraq you have to shoot the dogs. One of our staff sergeants got bit early on, and he had to have these rabies shots—like, the old-school ones with the six-inch needles. After that it was like a mandatory rule: You will shoot every dog.
>
> So we were clearing this whole village, nobody getting shot or dying, but it was chaos. Things were burning, yada, yada. We came to this last house and this dog was going crazy.
>
> Can I just shoot it?
>
> Oh yeah, absolutely.
>
> So I went over to the dog and shot next to it, just to scare it. The dog started to shake so uncontrollably, I thought it was going to die of a heart attack.
>
> Maybe I was too soft at the time . . . but I just had this feeling, like, what are we doing?

---

5. Watson, "Souls in Anguish Tortured by War Memories."

This dog was barking because a bunch of soldiers just went through its house and grabbed its owner and now they're breaking things.

What am I doing here? It was not a good feeling."[6]

Johnathan Shay provides the additional important insight that moral injury is best healed by veterans themselves with professionals providing a safe space in which the veterans can engage in telling their narratives to one another. It is the process of the veterans telling their stories that is the essence of their healing. Members of the healing professions can serve as trustworthy guides through the process and be empathetic listeners provided they listen with heart and head; make the process about the veteran; and are humble enough to understand that the veterans who have experienced the moral injuries have much to teach the professionals. In other words, it is the veterans themselves who are the agents of their own healing.[7]

In addition to the safe space, there must also be a sacred space to affect healing of moral injuries. Shame, guilt, alienation, and despair, that often attends to the first three, are profoundly spiritual or soul-related injuries and not simply psychological. What is a sacred space? Sacred means to be set aside for a holy or single purpose usually having to do with a religious use. Veterans often feel that what they have participated in as combatants is so morally reprehensible that there is no possibility for reconciliation and therefore they feel alienated from the divinity due to their moral failures. In order for there to be forgiveness or reconciliation there must be both a sacred space in which to confront the divinity and some means by which communication with the divinity is possible. We will discuss this vital matter of a safe and sacred space further in the final chapter.

Retired Navy Captain William Nash, a psychiatrist who headed the Marine Corps combat stress programs, says, "Forgiveness, more than anything, is key to helping troops who feel they have transgressed."[8] Moral wounds or injuries require something more than emotional or physical healing. Moral wounds are not medical issues, though they may manifest medical needs if left unattended. They are profoundly religious issues. Military chaplains see troops struggling with moral injury at the basic level of troops in the trenches. Soldiers wrestle with the notion of forgiveness even if they don't possess the religious language to describe their struggle.

6. Bebinger, Freemark, and Guntzel, "Moral Injury."

7. Shay, "Casualties."

8. See Nash et al., "Psychometric Evaluation of Moral Injury Events Scale."

Soldiers will frequently ask if they need to confess an action—or an inaction. All too frequently they come to their own conclusion that they have gone past the point of possible redemption and cannot accept the notion that God could or would forgive them. They adopt language that reflects their sense of alienation like: "I'm a monster." "It should have been me and not those good guys who died." "I'm not a hero. The guys who were killed are the real heroes." "If there is a God, he couldn't forgive what I've done." These are profoundly religious questions though they certainly are not limited to any single faith tradition.

The challenge facing faith communities and chaplains in uniform in particular is in finding a way to address the issue of moral wounds in a constructive fashion. There are many roadblocks in the way. It goes against the grain of a warrior's self-image to think that one cannot carry the weight of one's duty in combat. Ergo PTS is seen as a weakness, a failure on the part of the warrior. Likewise, moral injury implies an ethical failure by the warrior who serves in a force whose motto stresses honor, duty, and country. Equally problematic is the daunting challenge of determining how to help someone who believes that he or she cannot say what's bothering them for fear of losing one's security clearance or being declared unfit for duty.

Military chaplains must not only respond to and care for those warriors who have experienced moral injuries; they are also people who have suffered moral injuries themselves. The double challenge of experiencing personal moral injury combined with the demand to be a caregiver for others who have experienced moral injuries places a significant burden upon military chaplains and their families. In part due to the atmosphere of antireligious sentiment common in today's cultural milieu military chaplains have frequently adopted a medical model of responding to the moral injuries of others. That is to say, military chaplains have moved to seeing themselves as therapists, counselors, or healers who diagnose and treat "clients" in much the same manner as psychologists or clinical social workers. This tendency is one filled with potential problems for the military chaplain. In order to stay true to a vocational calling to tend to the spiritual well-being of themselves and others, chaplains must be well trained, grounded in their own faith traditions with well-honed skills in understanding the spiritual nature not only of the injuries experienced by themselves and others, but of the need to be well trained and deeply committed to their own spiritual core.

We do not suggest that there ought not be a relationship between the religious and the medical or other helping communities. Indeed, each community brings richness and essential aspects to the treating of both the physical, spiritual, and moral injuries incurred by warriors. Military chaplains must be able to possess and demonstrate a mature and well-developed personal spirituality that is deeply informed and shaped by the religious and theological tenets of their faith traditions.

Warren Kinghorn, who is both a professor of psychiatry and pastoral and moral theology at Duke University Divinity School, has analyzed and criticized the medical model that has come to predominate in the treatment of moral injury. Though insightful and clinically useful, psychological theories of moral injury are limited by their empirical suppositions. This makes them unable to treat the problem as anything other than a technical one. Thus, their empiricism makes for an inability to evaluate the moral suppositions and rules under attack in cases of moral injury. They are unable to distinguish between meaningful and non-meaningful moral suffering. "Communities and meaning-structures [religious communities and faith convictions] can be instrumental, but only instrumental" to the process of healing in moral injury. For Kinghorn, who sees moral injury in terms of moral and penitential theology, Christian communities need to make room for combat veterans to experience confession and absolution. They need a community that can walk with them on an honest path toward reconciliation, recognizing that we are all implicated in the violence of our world.[9]

Brock and Lettini tell the story of Herm, a chaplain during the Vietnam War. Herm witnessed the terrible impact of the war's atrocities upon the soldiers he served. "I was amazed," he said, "at their personal shame—not guilt—but profound, searing shame. Many felt that they had committed a personal affront against God." This sense of shame emerged especially when he had them read the Psalms, Psalm 51 in particular. At a time when moral injury was not yet named, Herm was drawn by these experiences to the conclusion that something far more profound than PTS was going on in the lives of these soldiers.[10] The power of this penitential psalm and the salutary effects of Herm's regular practice of serving communion with its promise of forgiveness and mercy and Jesus' solidarity in human suffering are surely lessons for today's growing awareness of moral injury.

9. Kinghorn, "Combat Trauma and Moral Fragmentation," 67–69.

10. Brock and Lettini, *Soul Repair*, 26–27.

Theological Reflections

The problem of evil is as familiar as it is seemingly insoluble. If God is gracious, just, and omnipotent, why is there evil? In theological terms it seems totally plausible to say that moral injury is an encounter with evil so radical that it evokes the problem of evil as a deeply existential reality rather than simply a theological conundrum. We are all familiar with the reality of evil within in us and around us. Given the webbed interconnectedness of all things, we cannot escape being touched by the manifestations of evil that permeate our world. The Law of God, says Helmut Thielicke, keeps reminding us of this truth of our worldly existence.

> It compels us to realize that, so long as we are here below, we are implicated in innumerable, suprapersonal webs of guilt . . . that we are actors in a thousand plays which we individually have not staged, which we might wish never be enacted, but in which we have to appear and play our parts.[11]

For Thielicke, then, ethics is not a matter of competing philosophical theories. It is a theological matter of how we cope morally and with hope in this in-between time, the time between the eschatological fulfillment of Christ's redemptive work and the lingering reality of terrible evil.[12] In other words it is life in the tension of the interplay between the accusation of God's Law, innately present in the brokenness of life, and the hope and promise of the gospel.

It is humanity's lot in general to live in this tension, to be caught in webs of suprapersonal guilt and placed on stage in tragic dramas not of our choosing. Recognizing this should place the faith community in a position of solidarity with those suffering moral injury. However, for the victims of moral injury their drama is a counsel of despair; there is only the accusing Law and no hint of gospel hope.

Providing help for those locked in the grip of despair is a pastoral task involving the chaplain along with the pastoral ministry of the community of fellow sufferers and of the caring congregation for those who have returned from battle struggling to reenter civilian life. It is important to provide a safe and welcome place in the church. Providing safe and sacred space for returning warriors to find healing for their wounds is an obligation of the churches and their congregations. No matter what their position

11. Thielicke, *Theological Ethics*, 436.
12. Ibid., 44.

on war may be, the unconditional demand of Christian love, which is the cornerstone of the Christian ethic, reaches out to all.

In terms of the just war tradition, which has been observed inside and outside the churches, the principle that a war to be just must be declared by a legitimate authority, means for a democratic society that the citizenry take ownership for that declaration and responsibility for its casualties, whether physical or spiritual, including all who share in the losses of war. The Christian church along with other faiths have a vocational obligation to lead the way in their own witness of caring.

In her recent book in which she relates stories of the morally injured with whom she has been embedded, Nancy Sherman is insistent throughout on the duty of society to take responsibility for the well-being of their returning service men and women. The nation and its noncombatant citizens have been in some measure responsible for the war by their political involvement, their taxes, and in various ways supporting the war. Thus she states emphatically,

> We have a sacred moral obligation to those who serve, whether or not we agree with the causes of those wars and whether or not those who serve agree with them. Those moral obligations are institutional, both governmental and nongovernmental: veterans are morally owed the best possible resources across the widest swath of medical psychiatric, social, legal, and technical services. But the obligations are also interpersonal, one-on-one. We have duties to each other for care and concern: normative expectations and aspirations that we can count on each other, we can trust and hope in each other, and we can be lifted by each other's support.[13]

Clearly, no mere ethical reflection on right and wrong will avail in and of itself. The awful encounter with evil, as Thielicke observed, is always for the Christian a deep theological question. A common theological response to the problem of evil is to posit that God in creating needed to allow for freedom if the creation is to have its own integrity. Out of love of creation the all-powerful God freely limits God's self. Characteristic of God's love for the creation is that willingness to be open to its rejection and, instead of coercing obedience, to suffer with the creation in order to redeem it.

This argument from love and freedom popular though it may be does not stop the nagging questions of why evil should emerge in the wake of

---

13. Sherman, *Afterwar*, 3.

freedom or even how much freedom for evil an omnipotent God can allow to go on. "How long, O Lord, How long?" This is the lament of the psalmist:

> How long, O Lord? Will you forget me forever?
>> How long will you hide your face from me?
> How long must I bear pain in my soul,
>> And have sorrow in my heart all day long?
> How long shall my enemy be exalted over me?
> (Ps 13:1–2)

The mystery persists. For this reason many theologians would have us look not to the mystery of evil's origin. ("Universal sin" for example has largely replaced "original sin"; the former describes a fact while origin remains a mystery.) Instead of looking to origins, some call us to consider what God in love for the troubled world is doing to redeem it from itself. Taking that advice we can begin to see some theological resources that can provide sustenance and a compass for those seeking to walk with the morally injured on the path to healing.

The Beatitudes with which Matthew begins Jesus' Sermon on the Mount give expression to characteristics of *agape* love's character and disposition. As "blessings" they are capacities born of that grace of God in Christ that engenders love.[14] In the second of the Beatitudes (Matt 5:4) we read, "Blessed are those who mourn for they shall be comforted." Mourning, the deep sense of loss and grief in the face of death, gives expression to love's profound relationality. This may be a response to the loss of someone near and dear but it may also be an empathetic response to the tragic loss of life in the world around us through acts of violence, the fury of natural disaster, or the terrors of war. The onset of mourning when confronted with such loss of life or, more broadly, with all manner of human suffering, tells us of our inherent connectedness with all in the community of life. Our grief and our empathic capacity to feel the pain of others is a testimony to that connectedness. It is a readiness to be in solidarity with the suffering. It is love reaching out to affirm those relationships with the hurting in a desire to comfort and heal.

Even as it is Jesus who announces and bestows these blessings of love's disposition, it is Jesus who embodies them in his life and work of self-giving love for all people. Jesus' solidarity with the suffering of our sad world comes to its most complete revelation in the event of the crucifixion. We

---

14. See Childs, *Ethics in the Community of Promise,* 46.

understand that in the mystery of the cross Jesus took upon himself the sinful brokenness of our world and even death itself. However, we must insist that, contrary to some traditional views, it was not simply the human Jesus who endured the burden of human sin and our death; it was an event in the very life of the Triune God. For Luther the unity of human and divine in the Christ and the unity of the Son with the Father and the Spirit made it clear that Christ's passion was indeed God's passion. Luther is quoted thus in the *Formula of Concord*, one of Lutheranism's confessional documents, "if it cannot be said that God died for us, but only a man, we are lost."[15] While the *Formula* makes clear that it is not in the nature of divinity to die, it is clear from Luther that the suffering and death of humanity as embodied in the suffering and death of the Christ is taken into the divine life of the Trinity united as the persons are in the mutual indwelling of one another in the bonds of love.

This theopassionism is central to Jürgen Moltmann's theology of the Trinity. These are his profound reflections on Jesus' cry from the cross, "My God, my God, why have you forsaken me!"

> If we take the relinquishment of the Father's name in Jesus' death cry seriously, then this is even the breakdown of the relationship that constitutes the very life of the Trinity: if the Father forsakes the Son, the Son does not merely lose his sonship. The Father loses his fatherhood as well. The love that binds the one to the other is transformed into a dividing curse. . . . Communicating love and responding love are alike transformed into infinite pain and into the suffering and endurance of death. . . . The Father "delivers" up the Son in order through him to become the Father of those who have been delivered up (Rom. 1:18ff.). The Son is given over to this death in order that he may become the brother and savior of the condemned and the cursed. . . . What happens on Golgotha reaches into the innermost depths of the Godhead, putting its impress on the trinitarian life in eternity.[16]

In Moltmann's account we begin to grasp the depth of divine solidarity with human suffering. There is no pain of human suffering—not even the pain of moral injury—that is not comprehended in God's experience of the cross. If the broken souls of the morally injured feel as though a meaningful universe has crumbled beneath their feet and left them bereft of hope,

---

15. Formula of Concord, Article VIII, 44.

16. Moltmann, *The Trinity and the Kingdom*, 80–81.

God has experienced this very thing in the rending of the relational unity of the divine life in whom the very world has its ground and sustenance. Sin itself is estrangement from God and one another. Moral injury is that estrangement brought to an extreme level of intensity. God has taken that estrangement into God's very life and suffered its terrors that in the power of divine love it may be overcome. In the final analysis, the almighty power of God is best understood as infinite and unfailing, steadfast love.

For the morally injured and those who seek to minister to them the vital truth of God's solidarity in our suffering is of central importance to the possibility that the healing of the spirit can occur. Moreover, the victory of the resurrection stands as the ultimate triumph of God's suffering love. This is the comfort promised in the Beatitude for those wounded ones who mourn the loss of their soul's vitality and it is the "comfort" in the sense of God's gracious support and strength for those who are called to serve the morally injured. All of these things we are saying are there in the means of grace, the sacraments, and the rite of repentance and absolution but they must be brought to life with pastoral sensitivity not only grounded in theological depth but also in a deeper understanding of the guilt and shame that are deeply a part of the morally injured.

Moral injury involves guilt and/or shame depending on the situation.[17] Brock and Lettini, quoted above, emphasize shame. Guilt may be understood in terms of experiencing the contradiction between who we are and what we should do. Shame can be understood as the contradiction between who we are and what we want to be.[18] The themes of lost trust and betrayal, of being cut off from one's self and one's relationships surface in the accounts of moral injury. "People often describe moments of intense shame with the words, 'I wanted to die,' as if to say that shame is so painfully confusing to one's existence that non-existence would be preferable."[19] Guilt and shame are rooted in our innate relationality as human beings. (Recall our previous discussion of creation in the image of God.) That is, their power is in their capacity to damage or virtually destroy our capacity for relationship and, thus, rob us of our very selves. "Our pastoral task concerning persons suffering from shame is to assist them to return from isolation to relationship."[20] Again, the means of grace are there to take pastoral

17. Sherman, *Afterwar*, 81–86.

18. Binau, "Shame and the Human Predicament," 132.

19. Ibid, 137.

20. Ibid, 143.

care beyond the capacity of those who minister. They are an assurance of God's radical and unconditional acceptance and one's unquestionable place in God's beloved human community. The mutual support of that community, we reiterate, must be sustained. Notwithstanding the unique aspects of combat traumas that bring on shame and guilt, it is possible for those who have not gone to war to relate at least at some level; most if not all of us have had experiences that cause feelings of guilt and shame. We may find renewal in divine grace and are able to move on. However, the memories of the events and the sense of guilt and shame that goes with them remain to haunt us, often on a sleepless night, when they come upon us unawares, triggered by some unbidden thought. The prodigal son of Luke 15:11–24 was restored to life by his father's gracious acceptance because he was restored to family, the locus of his true self, from the alienation of a life gone bad. No longer in thrall to a Gentile pig farmer and isolated from his authentic community, he nonetheless must still live with the lingering consequences of his wasted inheritance and the regrets of his actions.

The challenge of this ministry to the morally injured requires the kind pastoral and theological discernment that brings us back to the vital importance of critical thinking. The ability to think critically about each of the varied circumstances military chaplains find themselves confronting is an essential skill. While critical thinking is frequently implicit in theological education and training, it must become more explicit in the theological and spiritual formation of military chaplains. Just as other professional skills such as preaching, the interpretation of sacred texts, and worship practices are taught as subjects within the core curriculum of clergy, so must critical thinking be taught to clergy. Like the skills of surgical incision or diagnostic examinations for physicians, the skill of thinking critically for chaplains must also be developed in their preparatory training to function as professionals within their vocational areas. Nowhere is this more in demand than for the ministry to the morally injured.

Chapter Nine

Ethical Deliberation and the Ministry of the Chaplain

Preamble: The Just War Context

TOWARD THE END OF chapter 2 we gave some discussion to just war thinking and tradition. There we listed the basic principles of *jus ad bellum* and *jus in bello* along with a brief discussion of the traditional theological rationale and historical purpose of just war thinking in the history of Christian thought. There is no need to repeat this well-known material here. What we need to do is reflect upon the proposition offered there:

> *If jus ad bellum cannot be ethically justified there is no ground for jus in bello and the further ethical implications of its provisions. At the same time the failure of jus in bello in a given conflict can undermine the validity of just war claims based on the principles of jus ad bellum.*

On the face of it this statement is simply obvious: if there is no justification for just war theory it hardly makes sense to develop a military ethic involving the conduct of war. You would be attempting to develop ethics for an enterprise which is inherently unethical. Thus, there is a continual need to reevaluate just war theory in general and rigorously apply the criteria of *jus ad bellum* in every given instance where armed response is being considered. In the opinion of some it seems possible in a given conflict to argue that, though it is an unjust war, it is being conducted responsibly in accord with the principles of *jus in bello* and that this is the lesser of evils, at least for those on the receiving end of military action. Certainly, if war is underway that is reasonably considered unjust, one would hope that combatants and leadership would adhere to just conduct. Examples in recent history can be given. However, just conduct in war does not make the conflict a just war. Combatants who have tried to conduct themselves ethically in a conflict they come to consider unjust may find scant comfort in that fact. Nancy Sherman observes that deployed troops want "assurance that wars will be justified on moral or even prudential grounds . . . ." Such assurances may not be forthcoming during deployment with the result that "deep resentments may fester, and veterans may become re-traumatized as they live through new wars that they believe are unjustified or unnecessary."[1] The criteria of *ad bellum* and *in bello* are too deeply integrated with one another for the moral reality of the one not to interpenetrate the moral reality of the other.

It should be noted that *The Department of Defense Law of War Manual* insists that *jus ad bellum* and *jus in bello* operate independently of each other. However, their point does not contradict the connection we are making here. Rather, the *Manual* wants the distinction made clear in order to assure that compliance with *jus ad bellum* is required even in the absence of full compliance with *jus in bello* and *jus in bello* is required even in the absence of *jus ad bellum*.[2] This it seems to us is a mandate that is appropriate to our concerns but not engaged in the same sort of ethical reflection we are working on.

Clearly we have taken the position that just war thinking remains useful and sustainable even as we have to rethink the nature of war today. It remains a tool for navigating the tragic choices we may face in a hostile world. We have also indicated then that declaring a war just as a last resort in the face of aggression and grievous injustice does not make it any less tragic and embroiled in the evil of human inhumanity. Therefore, the approach we take to military ethics under the auspices of the just war tradition needs to recognize, as already suggested above, the constant ambiguity of moral choice in a broken world and the necessity of grace for the journey through it.

However, affirming the validity of just war thinking in general immediately creates the problem of having to apply its criteria to every conflict and, therefore, opens the door to selective conscientious objection. Luther, for example, who supported the long just war tradition, presented some thoughts that we might construe as affirmation of selective conscientious

---

1. Sherman, *Afterwar*, 47.
2. *Law of War*, 86–87, 3.5.

objection. "What if a prince is in the wrong?" he asks. "Are his people to follow him then too?" Luther says that the answer is "No" for one must obey God who desires the right rather than human leaders (Acts 5:29). Luther also recognizes that one may not be certain if the prince is right or wrong. In such cases if, after due diligence, the subject is still unable to know for sure, then that person is free to obey the prince without peril to their soul.[3]

Regardless of how one might interpret the relevance of Luther's counsel for today, Lutherans in America along with other Christian denominations have been on record in support of selective conscientious objection, a public position prompted by the turmoil over the Vietnam War. The following is from the 1973 study document produced by the former Lutheran Council in the USA. subsequent to testimony before the Senate Armed Services in February of 1971 on behalf of selective conscientious objection:

> US Lutherans of the three churches participating in the Lutheran Council [the American Lutheran Church, the Lutheran Church in America, and the Lutheran Church-Missouri Synod] have expressed as their official policy the position of support for selective conscientious objection—the individual's right to refuse participation in a particular war when such participation, to him, would clearly be wrong. The churches have asked the government to change the law so that selective objection is legal; they have also committed themselves to pastoral support of those who find themselves in conflict with law for reasons of conscience.[4]

On October 21, 1971 the United States Conference of Catholic Bishops issued their Declaration on Conscientious Objection and Selective Conscientious Objection. Having stated their respect for the consciences of those who serve in the armed forces and for those who are conscientious objectors or selective conscientious objectors, the bishops acknowledge the procedural complications of selective conscientious objection but still call on moralists, lawyers, and civil servants to work for a policy change that "can reconcile the demands of the moral and civil orders concerning this issue."[5] They reaffirm the recommendation made in their 1968 pastoral letter, "Human Life in Our Day," calling for:

---

3. Martin Luther, "Temporal Authority," 12–126.

4. *The Witness of U.S. Lutherans on Peace, War, and Conscience.*

5. United States Conference of Catholic Bishops, "Declaration on Conscientious Objection and Selective Conscientious Objection."

A modification of the Selective Service Act making it possible for selective conscientious objectors to refuse to serve in wars they consider unjust, without fear of imprisonment or loss of citizenship, provided they perform some other service to the human community....

However, the law has not been changed to accommodate such a choice. DoDI 1300.6 clearly states that conscientious objection to be recognized by the military must be objection to "war in any form." Thus 3.5.1 of 1300.6 states: "An individual who desires to choose the war in which he or she will participate is not a Conscientious Objector under the law. The individual's objection must be to all wars rather than a specific war."[6]

Here it seems we have an important example of how the respect for conscience in the free exercise of religion must still operate within the constraints of what the military considers essential to its mission. While this law against selective conscientious objection in today's voluntary armed services for the most part impacts service members who are potential combatants, chaplains again stand at the crossroads. They need to support the military's mission with their loyalty and their pledged service to military personnel and their families. However, in that very capacity they may well be called upon to provide pastoral care for a potential SCO with whose position they may feel some sympathy, especially given the fact that many Christian chaplains come from faith communities who have been on record in favor of selective conscientious objection and have even lobbied for changing the law prohibiting it. Whatever the case, the chaplain will of course minister to those who struggle with concerns of conscience over a given war or may have been court-martialed for refusal on grounds of conscience to participate in a specific war.

Whether or not a soldier is driven by conscience to suffer court martial for refusal to participate in what he/she considers an unjust cause, warriors do worry about the justice of the cause and struggle with their own participation and responsibility. This is the finding that philosopher and

6. Christopher J. Eberle, in a lengthy article arising from his experience teaching at the United States Naval Academy, has argued that "theists," people of religious faith, cannot commit to indiscriminate obedience, including obedience to legal orders in an unjust cause since obedience to God always transcends obedience to government. Officer candidates who hold such belief should not take the Oath of Commissioning unless they can somehow understand that oath to be valid only for just causes. Be that as it may, Eberle's concern is the moral validity of a faith-based or "theistic" argument in a context of public service. He claims no knowledge of the legal entailments. See "God, War, and Conscience."

psychoanalyst Nancy Sherman reached from her interviews with soldiers. They may not think in abstract terms about just war principles but they do worry about the goodness of the ends of their wars and if these outweigh the destruction they are a part of and "what they *do* worry about is whether they are going to war on a pretext for other actual causes. In a deep and personal way, they worry about whether they are being betrayed or manipulated by leadership, and how they can serve honorably in those circumstances."[7] Many it would seem resemble Luther's category of those who after diligent thought cannot be certain of the cause move forward out of duty. On the other hand, a deep sense of betrayal by leadership may render one a candidate for moral injury.

If the possibility of a just war in a particular case can be called to question and create a crisis of conscience for some facing participation in it, the phenomenon of moral injury alerts us to the possibility that the experiences of war—especially instances of dramatic violation of *jus in bello* principles—can lead people to conclude that the impossibility of real *jus in bello* vitiates just war theory as a whole. Of course, the conditions of modern warfare and contemporary battles against terrorists and insurgents have made the lines between combatant and noncombatant blurred or virtually invisible, prompting some to pronounce *jus in bello* obsolete on that account alone. Yet one wonders if it was ever really possible to spare noncombatants even in ancient times for the fallout from war upon civilians who suffered loss and privation in its wake is hard to ignore. That is no less true today for families grieving and torn apart and refugees fleeing the devastation.

Just war thinking remains an important construct, as long as we understand that the choice and prosecution of war is tragic. The theory exists then, as previously stated, to restrain the urge to war and constrain unbridled cruelty in the pursuit of war, realizing that under the best of conditions it is a cruel enterprise. We pray for and support those who fight and those loved ones who are a part of their sacrifice. We honor bravery and heroism. But we do not lionize war. Recognizing war's radical ambiguity, we reiterate that our ethical vision will be realistic about that and, based in our Christian faith, supported by the gospel promise of God-with-us even in the "valley of the shadow of death."

---

7. Sherman, *The Untold War*, 45–46.

Jus Post Bellum and Just Peacemaking

The doctrine of *jus post bellum* refers to the criteria for ending a war justly. In effect it is the other side of the coin of *jus ad bellum*. It seeks to be sure that the conflict has ended with justice having been done. It seeks to insure that those guilty of war crimes receive appropriate punishment and that the innocent are spared. Withal, *jus post bellum* requires that the "right intention" required by *jus ad bellum* be maintained, precluding the exacting of vengeance, or the greedy appropriation of territory or goods. Ending the war justly may also involve aid to the innocent victims of the defeated country and assistance in rebuilding. Clearly there is a good deal of judgment and interpretation required by the government of the victor nation or coalition of nations and room for debate as to what constitutes a just end to a given war. Delving more deeply into the subject of *jus post bellum* is not of immediate concern to our project. However, what is of immediate concern is the fact that governing authority is involved in just ending as it is in the decision to go to war. Taken together, *ad bellum* and *post bellum* point us in the direction of society and government's responsibility for just peacekeeping and just peacemaking.

In his forward to Sherman's *Afterwar* retired US Army General James M. Dubik places the work of caring for the morally injured that we discussed above as a part of *jus post bellum*. Furthermore, concern for the infinite value of those in harm's way means that the peacemaking of *jus post bellum* means taking seriously the fact that just war theory is designed to make it difficult to go to war:

> Losing a battle or engagement, fighting a battle that is unconnected to a larger purpose, being killed or maimed in an unjust, or imprudent, or unnecessary battle or war—any one of these can give rise to a sense of betrayal. . . . As human beings each of us has moral worth beyond our instrumental utility to a task or to society. Demanding that a soldier risks his or her life for no good reason is to treat that soldier as an object, not a human being. This is, perhaps, the ultimate moral injury, another manifestation of war's hellishness.[8]

In chapter 3 we said the following:

> This promise of God's future for the world weaves its way throughout the Old Testament, especially among the prophets. Against the

---

8. Sherman, *Afterwar*, xv.

backdrop of this long tradition of hope and expectation for the reign of God Jesus came preaching the nearness of God's kingdom. He identified his own person and work with the consummation of centuries of hope and longing for the reign of God to be manifest in its fullness.[9] Jesus' resurrection victory over sin and death became the ultimate fulfillment of God's covenant promises; in that victory the hoped for future was made present.[10] It is the future of the full realization of God's *Shalom*, the Hebrew word for "peace" that is all-encompassing as it includes wholeness, unity, justice, freedom, and the triumph of life.

This comprehensive notion of *shalom* is both the "good" at the heart of gospel promise and hope and the "good" whose values Christians strive for in love for all. These values of *shalom* direct the faith communities' advocacy for peace and justice.

The Christian community along with other faith communities is a part of the body politic with a responsibility for its policies and a voice in their formulation. We have already spoken of support for our warriors. Now we should add that they should not only be honored but they should also be heard. People in poverty should be consulted on the best ways to alleviate it. People with disabilities need to be consulted on the most effective ways to provide access to opportunity. People who know war and its devastation firsthand need to be heard about the necessity of keeping and making peace. The chaplains can be a link between the experience of the military and the faith communities they represent, helping them to engage the process of public policy on behalf of the things that make for peace.

The resources for Christian citizens as advocates for peace are there in documents of the church bodies. While recognizing that the church does not have uniquely Christian international policies or a divine or biblical politics for our time, the Evangelical Lutheran Church's social statement, *For Peace in God's World*, adopted in 1995, calls upon Christians to be active citizens in the affairs of government as these relate to ways that make for peace. This means bringing our realism about human sin to bear upon an assessment of the behavior of our own nation: "Sin's power often makes itself felt in arrogant self-righteous views of national identity, and in narrow,

9. See especially Luke 4:17–21 and Matthew 11:4–5. In both cases Jesus is presenting himself as the fulfillment of Messianic promises for God's deliverance in the prophet Isaiah.

10. See Wright, *The Challenge of Jesus*, esp. 53, 89, 131–37, and Pannenberg, *Jesus— God and Man*, 66–88.

short-term, and absolute views of national interest."[11] The statement calls upon Christians to be engaged in creating a culture of peace, which includes interfaith sharing, concern for the human rights of the oppressed, the needs of the poor, and a just economic order that includes respect for human dignity, the necessities of life, fair distribution of goods and burdens, and care for the sustainability of the ecosystem. These are just some of the ways that make for peace. Christians will disagree on how these values can be achieved in a complex and conflictual world, but it is important that the faith community be engaged in deliberation on the issues of peace, seeking the Spirit's guidance for its witness.

The Vatican II document *Gaudium et Spes* devotes its long concluding section to the matter of peacemaking. The following from paragraph 78 is a good summary of its basic thrust:

> Peace is not the mere absence of war or the simple maintenance of the balance of power between forces . . . it is called, rightly and properly, a work of justice. . . . Peace here on earth cannot be maintained unless the good of the human person is safeguarded, and men are willing to trust each other and share their riches of spirit and talent. If peace is to be established it is absolutely necessary to have firm determination to respect other persons and peoples in their dignity, and to be zealous in the practice of brotherhood. Peace is also the fruit of love . . . . Peace on earth born of love for one's neighbor, is the sign and the effect of the peace of Christ. . . . All Christians are thus urgently summoned to live the truth in love and to join all true peacemakers in prayer and work for peace.

The United Methodist Church in its statement, *Our Social Principles on War and Peace*, from the 2008 *Book of Discipline,* states that war is incompatible with Christ's teachings and example and should not be pursued as a foreign policy strategy. The moral duty of all nations is to seek peaceful means for the resolution of disputes. Christians should support conscientious objectors, offer humanitarian aid to victims of genocide, and advocate against aggressive military actions that put the lives of civilians at risk.

We have given just three examples of church proclamations on the faith communities' responsibility to be active advocates for the things that make for peace. The key is to make use of these resources in response to Jesus' command of neighbor love and its striving to anticipate penultimately God's ultimate *shalom.* ("Blessed are the peacemakers, for they will be called

---

11. Evangelical Lutheran Church in America, "For Peace in God's World," 4, A.

children of God" Matt 5:9.) It is important for chaplains and Christians in the military to be engaged by and with the churches in the moral deliberation on matters of public policy related to the goals of justice in the interest of peace. A good example is provided by this from a news release by James H. Thrall from the 2003 General Convention of the Episcopal Church USA entitled "Being a Peace Church in A World of War." Military chaplains and peace activists engaged in a forum on peacemaking. The forum included Bishop George Packard, the suffragan bishop for chaplaincies, including those of the military. The forum recognized that the destructive capacity of modern warfare made the decision to avoid war even more urgent. While all recognized that armed conflict may at times be unavoidable, Chaplain Kristina Coppinger urged that all should become involved in seeking ways that make for peace and noted that the majority of the military would much prefer being ambassadors for the cause of peace rather than simply the force that intervenes when peace fails.[12]

Although we are discussing peacemaking from the standpoint of our Christian calling, the necessity of interfaith cooperation is critical, especially in these times of sectarian strife. Hans Küng's book, *Global Responsibility: In Search of a New World Ethic*, seems even more needed today than in 1991 when it was first published. Two statements that he makes and develops fit in at this point: "No World Peace without Religious Peace" and "No Religious Peace without Religious Dialogue."[13] The responsibility to minister in the pluralistic environment of the military can be a laboratory for those chaplains whose theology allows them to become important resources to their faith communities for better understanding of other faiths and cooperation with them for the sake of peace and reconciliation. Even some Christian denominations that have been traditionally resistant to interfaith cooperation are beginning to see resources developed to promote more open attitudes in the future.[14] Military chaplains from these communions particularly can be important resources.

12. Thrall, "Being at Peace Church in a World of War."

13. Küng, *Global Responsibility*. The two statements are the headings and focus of discussion for sections beginning on 71 and 107 respectively.

14. Han, Metzger, and Muck have offered particular curricular recommendations for better preparing evangelical students for a pluralistic world. They seek to inculcate a greater measure of hospitality in dealing with those of other faiths than has been the practice of evangelical exclusivism. Their laudable effect illustrates the problem. See "Christian Hospitality and Pastoral Practices from an Evangelical Perspective."

Decision-Making: A Dialogical Approach

We are ready for further consideration of ethical deliberation grounded in the deepest convictions of the Christian faith. We have already said a great deal about the Christian ethic. In chapters 3 through 6 we have elaborated upon *agape*, neighbor love, as the foundation of this moral vision. We have discussed the threefold nature of *agape* as self-giving, universal in its outreach, and committed to reconciliation, the reunification of the estranged. We have sought to correlate these characteristics of *agape* with the commonly held values/virtues of the military services. In so doing virtues, values, and principles consistent with the dynamic of neighbor love have surfaced and their implications for conduct have been explored. We have seen that the Christ is the supreme exemplar of the love he commands and the author of the very grace that enables us to love, however imperfectly, in the lingering reality of our own sin and of the world that is our home. A model of ethical deliberation couched in these convictions, powered by divine grace and driven by love in a loveless world provides more than guidance for decision-making. It embodies an understanding of the radical ambiguity of life in general and the situations of combat and military life in particular. This is only consistent with biblical and Christian realism concerning the nature of humanity. At the same time this faith-based ethic proceeds in the strength of the gospel promise that God has redeemed us and called us to wade into the mire of a tragic world empowered by grace and divine companionship to do our best to show love and seek justice.

A faith-based ethic of this order can help to provide preparation for the complex, confusing, and deeply disturbing experiences one may expect to encounter in military life. As has already been suggested (see above, page 83), faith-based ethics are an integral part of pastoral care. Ethics training in this mode of thought is doing pastoral care and ethical guidance in advance of people's engagement with the issues as well as giving guidance in the crucible of decision. Such a blend of theology and ethics, pastoral care and ethical training, can be one source of fostering the sort of spiritual resilience that can help warriors deal better with the traumas they may face in combat.[15]

If a faith-based ethics can help prepare warriors for what they are likely to face and guide them in the process of facing it, the blend of theology,

---

15. See for example the following Canadian Army article: Morris, "Fostering Spiritual Resiliency in Warriors"; and the US Army article by Rob Schuette, "Spiritual Resiliency Helps Soldiers Weather Life's Traumas."

ethics, and pastoral care can, we hope, also be one helpful pathway for re-covery from moral injury. Perhaps it will help to know that in the moral life, in combat or otherwise, the reality of evil is inescapable but the promise of divine grace is unlimited and the triumph of love in the triumph of Christ is the ultimate victory. Perhaps the moral life driven by a faith-based ethic laced with gospel promise in the face of human sin can not only provide a way to decision and a guide to conscience but also a path to recovery from an onslaught of evil that allows no good choices, only tragedy. We hope so.

In an article dealing with ethical leadership in the armed services, George Mastroianni, a Professor of Psychology at the US Air Force Acad-emy, speaks of developments in military ethics training that stress the in-teraction of personal morality and situational factors in ethical decision. This kind of approach supplants traditional patterns of ethics training as indoctrination. Instead, he relates that,

> while still relying on the development of a commitment to shared values and the professionalism of the military as crucial elements in sustaining ethical conduct. . . .
>
> Traditional lectures are complemented by "dilemma training" which moves beyond the classroom to give the soldier realistic experience and practice making difficult judgments, often now taking place under combat-like conditions in simulated villages complete with actors playing the role of civilians and insurgents.[16]

As a psychologist, Mastroianni is interested in the sort of training that is most effective in producing the most consistent moral conduct in the throes of combat. He speaks of the army and marines using this dilemma training as a way of applying the idea of "muscle memory" to ethical con-duct.[17] The more practice, the more embedded the sense of right decision and action becomes. Certainly this approach is in line with a long tradition of case study and role-playing that has been a staple of ethics education. For the present, however, we simply want to note that the recognition that personal morality and situation reality interact in decision-making is an important departure from legalistic indoctrination, which easily breaks down under the pressure of complex, confusing , and morally ambiguous circumstances. The *process* of the decision-making model we are propos-ing lives in the same neighborhood while yet couched in the operative

16 Mastroianni, "The Person-Situation Debate."

17. Ibid.

theological assumptions about the moral life that we have been advancing from the outset.

The idea of ethical "muscle memory" is important for appropriating any model of ethical deliberation. Real life and military life in particular does not always permit time for deliberation. Therefore, practicing the commended approach to ethical deliberation through case study and, if you will, "dilemma training," is needed so that the guiding ideas become embedded in one's consciousness. In this sense persons are preparing decisions in advance of challenges they will likely face. At the same time, there are certainly eventualities in which there is time for reflection and deliberation of the decision, as in the case of Col. Couch's decision, or in analyzing the aftermath of a particularly difficult morally charged episode, as in the case of Dr. Bradley's analysis based on the Semrau case.

Dialogical Ethics and the Ethics of Love

Ethically responsible conduct is frequently if not most often a matter of habit requiring little or no reflection. However, we focus here on the many cases that require deliberation and decision. In this regard, all ethics are situational in the sense that one must understand the peculiar features of the situation that calls for decision in order to act responsibly. In short, ethical decision is a matter of bringing ethical principles into dialogue with the situation at hand in order to discern what the best possible choice is. The general principles we have already identified and discussed to some degree as consistent with *agape* or neighbor love are: *respect for autonomy, sanctity of life, justice, promise-keeping, and truth-telling.* Because these principles are "general" and do not prescribe specific action for all situations, their demands need to be discovered in dialogue with the salient facts of the situation. This is a process of interpretation, of discernment common to a variety of ethical systems. For the Christian it is a process driven by love's desire to honor its call to care about the neighbor in response to Christ's command, even in the midst of the radically ambiguous situations of armed conflict. We recall Thielicke's distinction between philosophical ethics that begins with the task while Christian ethics begins with the gift: the grace to love.

Because all ethics are situational, demanding a careful assessment of what ethical challenges the circumstances pose, the previous discussion of critical thinking comes to the fore. Ethical decision requires the ability to discern what is going on, what are the key facts. What ethical issues do the facts present? What are the real possible alternatives? The ideal or desired choice might not be a possible choice when presented with a complex situation such as we saw in Bradley's discussion of the Semrau case. Only then can one begin to discern what love demands; how the seemingly relevant principle should be applied in decision and action.

One way in which the dialogue proceeds might be described as an exercise in intuitive discernment. Here we imagine a situation that is not complex in the sense of presenting a number of uncertain choices. Rather, it requires an immediate sense of what the other really needs. For the chaplain as pastor this is a constant demand: how best does one keep one's promise to minister and to respect the dignity and autonomy of the one presenting a need? It requires a readiness to listen carefully to find out as best as possible what the real need is and respond accordingly. It may mean honoring the sanctity of life by seeking a means for healing (recall our discussion of moral injury) or it may mean a confrontation that tells the truth in love. This artful capacity for discernment may be especially critical when chaplains are ministering to those outside their own faith tradition; the challenge is not only to discern true personal need but also to understand how meeting that need may be related to deeply held religious convictions.

Most challenging ethical decisions involve dealing with some sort of conflict: the claims of the parties calling for love's response are in conflict with one another or the obligations of one general principle are in conflict with those of another. The case analysis by Col. Bradley is illustrative: the life of the enemy combatant, the well-being of his comrades, the mission's importance, and the matters at stake in its successful completion represent potentially conflicting claims upon an ethically sound command decision. The resolution of conflicting moral claims requires critical thinking, and intuitive discernment as well. However, it is also helpful to consider a number of axioms which can provide some guidance in the resolution of conflicting claims. One might call them "adjudicating axioms."[18]

The first of these is *distinguishing between interest and need*. Some conflicting claims made upon individual or corporate ethical decision may be decidedly unequal because one is the expression of an interest on behalf of the individual or the collective whereas the other claim is more clearly a need. When such a distinction can be drawn, the meeting of need trumps the claims of interest. Though interests may not be perverse or selfish,

18. See Thomas, *Christian Ethics and Moral Philosophy*, 441–44.

neighbor love gravitates to the real needs of people when the values of life, wholeness, freedom, justice, and peace are at stake. Demands being made in the arena of public policy making are often distinguishable in terms of interests versus needs. We are tempted to cynicism when we see the inordinate influence of lobbyists for special interests prevailing over those whom we consider advocates for genuine needs. At the same time we also have cause to celebrate those public policies that do seek to meet real needs, for example, for food safety, drug safety, increased equal opportunity, public safety, and a wide variety of social welfare provisions.

When we think of this axiom in terms of just war theory, the connection is clear. While national "interest" can be a genuine need in defense of homeland and freedom, the sense of "interest" in the logic of this axiom is one where a country is seeking a self-aggrandizing gain. Just wars need to have a just cause rather than an aggressive quest for territory or resources.

The second approach to the resolution of conflicting claims is the practice of *limitation* or *modification*. In some situations the problem of conflicting claims and the obligations they entail can be resolved by limiting or modifying the response to those competing claims. This can be construed simply as the process of compromise. In our nation's public policies this has historically been the way legislators have sought in their budgeting decisions to respond to the multiple needs of the people, all of which cannot be fully satisfied in every case. Through taxation individual freedoms for economic gain are compromised to some degree in order to meet the varied demands of the common good. The same process happens, of course, at state and local levels.

Applying this axiom to the just war theory, the principle of last resort comes immediately to mind. When faced with the threat or reality of unjust conduct on the part of a nation, the obligation to maintain peace as opposed to war and the obligation to promote justice are in tension. If it can be determined that war is not a last resort, a modified response to curtail unjust actions such as economic sanctions and international inspections, as was done in Iraq before the outbreak of the war, may be the ethically responsible choice.

In some cases hard choices between competing obligations can be made by distinguishing which claim represents *the higher need or value*. For example, in matters of national security truth-telling will often take a backseat to preserving secrets judged to be critical to safeguarding lives and the legitimate interests of national security. In everyday encounters we are sometimes confronted with questions that we fear will be hurtful to someone if answered truthfully and we may decide that protecting that person from hurt is the higher need.

Peter French relates a situation faced by a Navy chaplain that fits here. The chaplain in question, when a young lieutenant, witnessed the senior chaplain inappropriately touching a female servicewoman. The woman subsequently came to him and told him she was going to bring charges for sexual harassment against the senior chaplain because, she said, this kind of behavior has gone on too often. Her request was that he stand by her in that process. Knowing that this was risky for his career, he nonetheless agreed to support her claim. While the senior chaplain was eventually disciplined the young chaplain was transferred to a lesser post and passed over for promotion despite a lack of any poor fitness reports.[19] The young chaplain decided that the higher need was justice for women in the service rather than his own security. Whistle-blowers in all walks of life—business, industry, education, government, and the military—have had to face the question of the higher need. Not uncommonly their choices for the truth have been costly to their own well-being. The Rand Corp. survey of sexual abuse in the military for 2014 "found that 62 percent of women who experienced a sexual assault and reported it endured some type of retribution or retaliation. . . . Social retaliation accounted for the largest form of perceived retribution, but 32 percent said they faced professional retaliation and 35 percent an adverse administrative event after reporting an incident."[20]

In terms of just war theory, the principles of last resort, just cause, and proportionality can all entail consideration of determining the higher need. Decisions under the auspices of these principles may also turn on the use of the final adjudicating axiom, *inclusiveness*. Much like the classic principle of utility, inclusiveness seeks to resolve conflicting choices by determining which decision will benefit the most people involved. The danger here is that one might bypass a higher need or obligation for the sake of the greater number. Insofar as this axiom resembles the principle of utility, the greatest good for the greatest number, it shares the classic problem of utilitarianism: the good of the many may come at the cost of injustice for the few. We provide two cases in the next chapter will test the use of the *inclusivity* axiom in the adjudicating of conflict as well as the possible preferred application of others.

19. French, *War and Moral Dissonance*, 23.

20. Kime, "Incidents of Rape in Military Much Higher than Previously Reported."

Chapter Ten

Three Cases in Conflict Resolution

Drone Warfare

SOME MAY ARGUE THAT the greater number of combatants is benefited by the use of drone warfare that keeps them out of harm's way, fewer "boots on the ground" and fighter pilots in the air. Some have also argued that there are fewer victims of collateral damage than in, for example, conventional bombing. Moreover, the special task force to study US drone policy launched by the Stimson Center, a Washington, DC-based think tank, expressed its belief that drone strikes do not cause disproportionate civilian casualties.[1] Despite comparisons with other forms of air strikes and the conclusion of the Stimson Center task force, opponents of the current uses of drone warfare question the moral strength of this claim. In a 2013 article it was estimated that 1,000 civilians were killed in drone strikes in Iraq and Afghanistan. That is one third of the total number of drone fatalities. Moreover, beyond civilian death and injury is the emotional and psychological toll on the populations in target zones. People there have reported hearing the drones twenty-four hours a day; they live in terror of them.[2] While the Stimson task force does not make this precise point, it does observe the danger that even a relatively few civilian casualties can arouse the anger of affected communities. The consequence can well be that such

---

1. *Recommendations and Report*, 10. Despite the title using the term "drone," the report consistently uses the term "unmanned aerial vehicles" or UAVs. We stick with the term *drone* for the sake of consistency.

2. Holt, "Hellfire from Above." So also Lauritzen, "'Lawful but Awful.'"

anger is turned into an effective terrorist recruiting tool, thereby potentially perpetuating hostilities.[3]

A further concern arises in the area of the *jus in bello* principle of noncombatant immunity is the definition that has been used for who is considered a combatant. Critics have contended that what started out as a drone campaign against those clearly a threat to US security has been expanded to classify all males of military age as combatants in zones of perceived threat.[4] To the degree that this policy is carried out, the distinction between combatant and noncombatant is called to question by what a counterterrorism official called the growing elasticity of the definition of combatant.[5] The Stimson task force report recognizes the changed circumstances of fighting non-state terrorists and the difficulty of that war by conventional standards of warfare.

> The legal norms governing armed conflicts and the use of force look clear on paper but the changing nature of modern conflicts and security threats has rendered them almost incoherent in practice. Basic categories such as "battlefield," "combatant," and "hostilities" no longer have a clear or stable meaning. When this happens the rule of law is threatened. The United States was founded on the rule of law principles, and historically has sought to ensure that its own actions, international law and the actions of foreign states are consistent with these principles. Today, however, despite the undoubted good faith of US decision-makers, it would be difficult to conclude that US targeted strikes are consistent with core rule of law norms.[6]

If one argues for the use of drones on the basis of the greater good of our forces through lesser risks and, in the belief of some, that there are also fewer civilian casualties, one of the criticisms is that these very considerations threaten to make the principle of last resort less urgent and the choice for war easier to make. The Stimson task force warns that drones could "create a slippery slope leading to continual or wider wars . . . they may lower the bar to enter a conflict, without increasing the likelihood of a satisfactory outcome."[7] As one theologian put it, "Drones are particularly dangerous as

---

3. *Recommendations and Report,* 10.

4. Rice, "War Crimes and Misdemeanors"; Coll, "Remote Control."

5. Rice, "War Crimes and Misdemeanors."

6. *Recommendations and Report,* 12.

7. Ibid, 11.

they tempt us, as well as other nations, to consider war 'easy' and 'cheap.' The age of drones, unless checked, will be the age of permanent war."[8]

Some critics have also likened the drone pilot's job as something like playing a video game that dispenses death from thousands of mile away with no threat to the pilot him or herself. While the drone pilots are out of harm's way in terms of physical danger, they see quite vividly the gory results of hitting the targets. As a consequence PTSD and moral injury have afflicted them as well.[9] Serious observers of drone warfare would never compare it to playing video games. In an interview with NBC News, former drone operator Brandon Bryant speaks of being haunted by his part in more than 1,600 deaths. He related what he witnessed on his screen at a Nevada air force base after the missiles his team fired hit their three targets:

> "The guy was running forward, he's missing his right leg . . . . And I watch this guy bleed out and I mean, the blood is hot." As the man died his body grew cold, said Bryant, and his thermal image changed until he became the same color as the ground. "I can see every pixel," said Bryant, who has been diagnosed with post-traumatic stress disorder, "if I just close my eyes.[10]

The Stimson task force declined either to glorify or demonize the use of drones. Their concern is their just deployment, appropriate oversight, and transparency concerning their use. Theologian Daniel M. Bell Jr. echoes this perspective in his published remarks. For him the use of drones is not intrinsically immoral. It is, he says, a matter of character—how are they used in a just and responsible way? Thus, he concludes:

> Therefore, the moral challenge of unmanned predator drones is this: Is the church teaching the virtues and Christian discipline of just war doctrine needed to use such technology and weaponry not merely effectively and efficiently, but also to use it wisely?[11]

In a sense, Bell's assessment and concern points to the purpose of our discussion. Drones are here to stay. The debate over their use and the effects of their proliferation internationally is an ongoing discussion. Our

8. The comments of Susan Brooks Thistlethwaite quoted in Holt, "Hellfire from Above," 22.

9. See Watson, "Military Drone Operators."

10. Engel, "Former Drone Operator Says He's Haunted." See also Keizer, "Stop drone strikes and the moral injury of their pilots."

11. Bell, "Let Character Prevail."

discussion of the matter is simply illustrative of how just war principles and proposed axioms for navigating ethical conflict might work together in addressing the ethical questions associated with drone warfare. Of course, neither chaplains nor the church are policy makers. However, they minister to those involved in drone warfare and must address the doubts and emotional fallout for these warriors. Moreover, the church as public church has not only the teaching duty and character formation duty that Bell commends; it's members have a public voice in our country's conduct of war.

Whether we are talking about drone warfare or other issues of military ethics the combined use of just war principles and axioms for adjudicating ethical conflict are part and parcel of seeking what ethicists would call "the burden of proof." That is to say that when a principle must be violated or set aside in favor of another, one must establish a burden of proof for doing so. Just war principles are a demand to show the burden of proof for violating the sanctity of life in killing that war entails.

Human Dignity and the Question of Torture

We have already discussed the case of Lt. Col. Stuart Couch, the Marine lawyer who refused to prosecute a suspect at Guantanamo because he was convinced that the man had been tortured. We recall that, despite Col. Couch's loyalty to the service and the country and desire to prosecute this terrorist, he was moved to his decision by his priest's comments on the innate dignity of all human beings and the consequent conviction that that divine precept is violated by torture. It is, as we have observed, a divine precept because it is grounded in biblical anthropology; the creation of humanity in the image of God. As such, the innate dignity of all persons is a dignity given by God; it can neither be acquired by our own efforts nor can it abrogated by our actions or the actions and judgments of others. Love's principles of respect for autonomy and the sanctity of life are corollaries of the dignity of each human life as understood in terms of humanity's creation in and destiny for fulfillment in the image of God.

The biblically based understanding that humanity's fulfillment in the image of God is an eschatological promise of the resurrection at the arrival of the kingdom of God is of critical importance here. In the Hebrew Scriptures the designation "image of God" refers to humanity's creation as recorded in Genesis 1:26–27 and echoed in 5:1–3 and 9:6. In the New Testament the phrase "image of God" is predominantly a reference to the divinity of Jesus, the Christ. A notable example is the testimony of Col. 1:15–20:

> He is the image of the invisible God, the firstborn of all creation; for in him all things in heaven and on earth were created, things visible and invisible, whether thrones or dominions or rulers or powers—all things have been created through him and for him. He himself is before all things, and in him all things hold together. He is the head of the body, the church; he is the beginning, the firstborn from the dead, so that he might come to have first place in everything. For in him all the fullness of God was pleased to dwell, and through him God was pleased to reconcile to himself all things, whether on earth or in heaven, by making peace through the blood of his cross.

However, though we can speak of the image of God in reference to God present in Jesus the Christ, we are also led to see that the risen Christ is the prototype of true humanity in the fullness of the divine image. Paul tells us in 2 Corinthians 3:18 that we are being transformed according to his image, that of the Christ, which is to say, *according to the image of God*. In 1 Corinthians 15:42–49 we discover that the ultimate transformation, humanity's fulfillment in the image of God is in the resurrection:

> So it is with the resurrection of the dead. What is sown is perishable, what is raised is imperishable. It is sown in dishonor, it is raised in glory. It is sown in weakness, it is raised in power. It is sown a physical body, it is raised a spiritual body. If there is a physical body, there is also a spiritual body. Thus it is written, "The first man, Adam, became a living being"; the last Adam became a life-giving spirit. But it is not the spiritual that is first, but the physical, and then the spiritual. The first man was from the earth, a man of dust; the second man is from heaven. As was the man of dust, so are those who are of the dust; and as is the man of heaven, so are those who are of heaven. Just as we have borne the image of the man of dust, we will also bear the image of the man of heaven.

In the Christ, in accordance with his true humanity, we see our own destiny, the prototype of true humanity, for Christ is the first resurrected one: Christ has been raised from the dead, the first fruits of those who have died" (1 Cor 15:20). The church's creed declares the unity of the divine and human in the Christ. This doctrine of the incarnation is confirmed by Jesus' resurrection. The incarnation embodies by analogy humanity's destiny as image of God, the fulfillment of creation, unity with God and with humanity in the bonds of love.

The universal sin of humanity is not that the image has been lost or impaired. It is more profound than that; it is to be in rebellion against God's destiny for humanity, the peace of unity with God and others in the bonds of love. So we live in the in-between time: our future is revealed already in the risen Christ but the ultimate future of God has not yet arrived. The promise of the creation narratives of Genesis is fulfilled in the promise of the risen Christ. For our purposes, this theological reflection on biblical anthropology is to make clear that human dignity is sealed for all in God's acts of creation and redemption. It remains the destiny of all.

We turn now to Paul Lauritzen's excellent book, *The Ethics of Interrogation: Professional Responsibility in an Age of Terror.*[12] Lauritzen offers a well-researched and probing examination of the complex ethical and legal limits of involvement in interrogation of prisoners by professionals in the areas of psychology, law, and, medicine. The context for this investigation is principally the interrogations conducted at Guantanamo Bay during the Bush administration. What is of special interest for us is the discussion toward the end on identifying a standard for judging what forms of interrogation techniques are morally acceptable.

The comments of Alberto Mora, former General Counsel of the Navy, regarding interrogation at Guantanamo Bay, serve as a fitting preamble. Mora opposed the coercive or "enhanced" interrogation practices that were authorized and carried out at Guantanamo. He regarded them as both unlawful and contrary to the values and character of the military and of an American society that has inculcated in its soldiers values that are contrary to mistreatment of other human beings.[13] In an interview with the *New Yorker* he was asked if there was a distinction between torture and cruel or degrading treatment. His answer:

> To my mind there is no practical or moral distinction. . . . If cruelty is no longer declared unlawful, but instead is applied as a matter of policy, it alters the fundamental relationship of man to government. It destroys the whole notion of individual rights. The Constitution recognizes that man has an inherent right, not bestowed by the state or laws, to personal dignity, including the right to be

12. Lauritzen, *The Ethics of Interrogation.*
13. Ibid., 161.

free of cruelty. It applies to all human beings, not just in America—
even those designated as "unlawful enemy combatants."[14]

While his argument is based on the Constitution and its roots in natural
law, it fits with the implications of the theological anthropology offered
above. The final comment in this quote that the inherent dignity of all and
their right to freedom from cruelty applies even to those who are considered unlawful enemy combatants is noteworthy. It speaks forcefully against
the posture of "moral exclusivism" that demonizes the other and considers
them outside the bounds of humane consideration. This we noted earlier is
at odds with the universality of *agape's* commitment to the neighbor. (See
above, p. 40.)

Lauritzen turns then to the Universal Code of Military Justice and
the Geneva Conventions. From these documents it appears clear that the
standard for what is ethically acceptable or unacceptable in interrogation
techniques is whether or not it violates human dignity. Lauritzen draws a
distinction between comparative and noncomparative dignity. "A noncomparative account of dignity embraces the idea that humans have an intrinsic
dignity that cannot be lost because it does not rest on any set of capacities or functions that might themselves be lost."[15] The theological account
of dignity rooted in the image of God is such a noncomparative account.
Lauritzen quotes Gilbert Meilander's view that we may not in fact be able
to make sense of a noncomparative view of human dignity apart from the
religious beliefs that formed it.[16]

Lauritzen argues that it is the comparative conception of human
dignity that is relevant to assessing the moral status of interrogation techniques. The comparative account he wishes to work with is grounded in
autonomy even though he acknowledges that a consideration of autonomy
does not exhaust all we would want to say about human dignity. Autonomy
entails the freedom to make informed responsible choices. We have seen
that respect for autonomy is a principle of neighbor love grounded in the
image of God. For Lauritzen respect for autonomy is a corollary of Kant's
statement that one should treat no one as a means to an end but always
as persons who have their own ends and goals. In Lauritzen's view those
interrogation practices that strip prisoners of their autonomy are ethically
unacceptable. Applying this standard, he believes that of the techniques

14. Quoted in ibid., 162.

15. Ibid., 184.

16. Ibid.

used at Guantanamo, forcing prisoners into sustained stress positions, sleep deprivation, and placing insects in the detainee's confinement box are abusive and waterboarding, is torture.[17]

What we have seen from Lauritzen's narrative of the policies on interrogation techniques during the Bush administration leads one to believe that an "ends-justifies-the-means" type of teleological ethic was at work. Terrorism and terrorists threaten the lives of Americans; any means that can elicit information that might thwart terrorist activities is therefore legitimate. Ethical structures that guarantee justice and fundamental human rights were judged by some in the military to have been set aside. Witness the testimony of Alberto Mora and his appeal to values foundational to the military, the Universal Code of Military Justice, the Geneva Conventions, and the tradition of *jus in bello* that precludes the use of torture. Lauritzen's appeal to Kant in defense of autonomy as a hallmark of human dignity evokes a deontological approach in contrast to the sort of teleological thinking operative at Guantanamo.[18]

Clearly the concern for justice and human dignity correlates with *agape*'s principles of respect for autonomy, the sanctity of life, and justice. Yet we have realized that the world is conflictual and often ambiguous. We have recognized that the obligations of love, as defined by one principle, may be in conflict with that of another or the appeal of one party can be in conflict with the appeal of another. Returning then to our axioms for conflict resolution, let's ask which approach would seem most defensible.

The conflict posed in the use of interrogation techniques is one between protecting American lives against the threat of terrorism versus practicing justice and/or respect for autonomy in safeguarding the dignity

---

17. Ibid., 185–187. Chapters 5 and 6 of Nancy Sherman's book, *The Untold War*, deal with interrogation and torture and provide hands-on commentary from those involved. This quote from an article written by one of her interviewees, a former interrogator, fits nicely with Lauritzen's conclusions: "I had learned never to dehumanize my enemy, but to maintain a concrete understanding of him as a human being" (134). The Army's interrogation manual, *Human Intelligence Collector Operations,* prohibits waterboarding, hooding, putting duct tape over eyes, inducing hypothermia, and forcing the detainee to be naked, perform sexual acts, or pose in a sexual manner. Military police are not to be ordered to "soften up" detainees and military working dogs are not to be used in interrogation. Cited in Skerker, *An Ethics of Interrogation*, 149.

18. Michael Skerker also regards the justification put forward in the interrogations of Guantanamo was a teleological one, i.e. a consequentialist argument vitiated by the fact that the data on the consequences of coercive torture were chronically ambiguous. *An Ethics of Interrogation*, 204–5.

of prisoners or detainees. This is clearly not a matter of *interest versus need*; the claims of the sanctity of life and justice/respect for autonomy are both "needs." One could argue that protection of lives through extracting vital intelligence by any means, including enhanced interrogation techniques that are either abusive or qualify as torture, is the *higher need or value*. But, to recur to the principles of just war, if we concur that abusive and torturous techniques violate provisions of the Uniform Code of Military Justice, the Geneva Conventions, and provisions of *jus in bello*, then we have to ask is the use of harsh interrogation techniques the "last resort"? When one raises the question of last resort the usual approach to conflict resolution is to employ what we have spoken of as the axiom of *modification or compromise*. The use of coercive but not abusive interrogation enables the military to gain important intelligence without at the same time violating its own principles of respect for human dignity and inflicting prisoners with abuse or torture. Some have argued that techniques that are not abusive are in fact more effective. However, that debate is outside the scope of our project.[19]

The point we need to make is that the reality of interrogation in the face of terrorism is yet another manifestation of our broken world. Consequently, even taking the path that leads away from abuse and torture does not mean that we are not caught up in the tragedy and ambiguity of deadly conflict. The use of adjudicating axioms is simply a compass for navigating this tragic state of affairs. From the standpoint of faith it is a question of how the principles that embody love of neighbor can best be served when, in fact, they cannot be perfectly served. In the face of this truth we recognize that the practice of the Christian ethic does not operate with the certitude of moral perfection but rather with the assurance of God with us with grace for the way.

Truth-Telling

Nancy Sherman relates the story of her conversation with a high-ranking Navy officer. "He told me that one of the most valuable lessons he learned

19. Michael Skerker has provided cases and analysis that give credence to the conviction that the use of torture provides unreliable intelligence and noncoercive means have often proven to be more effective in gaining cooperation. Indeed, the impermissibility of torture is no hindrance to the government's cause for the very reason that it is so unreliable as a means of gaining intelligence. Those tortured, if they don't die from it or go into shock, will likely say anything to get it to stop. His account of the US use of torture during the Bush administration is chilling. Ibid., 207–13. See also Stone, "Beyond Torture."

as an elite aviator came from the grueling, postmortem critiques after flight operations. The critiques lasted longer than any of the flights. A productive group review often depended on a unit leader prepared to acknowledge mistakes before subordinates."[20] The leadership of that unit evidently created an atmosphere and a practice in which honesty was possible and the benefits of truth-telling followed. Earlier we related Peter French's account of the young lieutenant chaplain who stood by his female colleague in her case against the senior chaplain. Like whistle-blowers in all walks of life, he paid a price. Corporations, recognizing the threat people feel in the face of telling the truth about something that seems wrong and recognizing the value of knowing the truth, have in many cases created avenues for truth-telling such as hotlines, special board committees, and ombudsmen. They have established structures that enhance the possibility for truth to be told and its benefits realized. Telling the truth and fostering an atmosphere in which truth-telling is possible are linked. Those responsible for circumstances that make honesty difficult or threatening in a real sense share responsibility with the liar for the lies told or the truth withheld.

According to recent study revealing widespread dishonesty among Army officers, creating an environment that encourages truth-telling is a work in progress for at least this branch of the military.[21] One captain reported that the number of tasks required at one point "went through the roof." Getting the whole formation to take an online training course with the problem of computer availability and the pressure of other demands led to a dishonest solution that officers came to see as necessary under the circumstances. "For a nine-man squad, they would pick the smartest dude, and he would go and take it nine times for the other members of his squad and then that way they had a certificate to prove they had taken it."[22] Examples of lying such as this are matched in the report by examples of deceit concerning compliance with directed actions.

> According to a senior officer, "A command inspection is required within 90 days of company command. People don't do it. They make it up." One Colonel spoke of inaccurate reporting following and undesirable directive. "We were asked to go to off-post housing to check on soldier quality of life. Folks were uncomfortable going so they pencil-whipped it." In the words of another senior

20. Sherman, *Untold War*, 25.

21. Wong and Gerras, *Lying to Ourselves*.

22. Ibid., 8.

officer, "We have levied [on us] so many information demands that we infer that if I'm not asked for specifics, they don't care. So, I'll just report ambiguous info."[23]

When the researchers asked the views of those on the receiving end of inaccurate data, they found a general acceptance of the fact that the data is wrong. "Nobody believes the data; [senior leaders] take it with a grain of salt," said one staff officer. Another one added, "We don't trust our compliance data. There's no system to track it." Officers admit to sending on what the Army institution wants to hear but is not totally honest. There is the case of reciting a mutually agreed deception but all concerned are willing "to sanction and support the illusion that all is well."[24]

The report goes on to cite instances that show many of the same issues of dishonesty occur in the combat environment as in the garrison context. "For example, a senior officer described how the combat mission can lead to putting the 'right spin' on reports: 'We got so focused on getting bodies to combat that we overlooked a lot of issues like weight control, alcohol, or PT [Physical Training].'" Also overlooked were training requirements such as sexual assault prevention. Still another officer reported on how supply accountability could be manipulated in a combat zone by lying about the need to replace lost equipment that was never actually lost; the budget for the combat zone is virtually infinite.[25]

The examples just given and many others included in the report are evidence of what the authors call "ethical fading."

> Ethical fading allows us to convince ourselves that considerations of right or wrong are not applicable to decisions that in any other circumstances would be ethical dilemmas. This is not so much because we lack a moral foundation or adequate ethics training, but because psychological processes and influencing factors subtly neutralize the "ethics" from an ethical dilemma. Ethical fading allows Army officers to transform morally wrong behavior into socially acceptable conduct by dimming the glare and guilt of the ethical spotlight.[26]

Thus, in face of a deluge and exponential growth of annoying administrative demands for compliance, many officers regard lying to the system as

23. Ibid., 10.
24. Ibid.12.
25. Ibid., 14–15.
26. Ibid., 17.

"prioritizing, accepting prudent risk, or simply good leadership."[27] The excuses offered by officers reflect this outlook. Having considered the reporting requirements as unreasonable, a less than totally truthful response can be considered a resistance to injustice in the system. "Officers convince themselves that instead of being unethical, they are really restoring a sense of balance and sanity to the Army." [28]

Two other justifications for dishonesty that may appear more compelling are claims that it was necessary to accomplish the mission or to support the troops. Fudging on what is deemed inessential is simply the sort of ethical compromise one must make to serve the overriding task of the mission. "I'm just going to 'check this box' . . . and if I'm 70 percent accurate, that's good enough to 1) keep my guys out of trouble and 2) keep my boss out of trouble so we can keep doing good things for the country." Or, perhaps a more persuasive or maybe disturbing example is that of a captain whose platoon leader and his replacement were both injured by an improvised explosive device. Rather than submit both to the required traumatic brain assessment, which would leave the platoon without leadership, he falsified the report. Leaving the men without leadership, he argued, would "put my boys in bags. . . . That ain't happening. I owe the parents of this country more than that."[29]

Perhaps many of the examples presented in the report could be construed as a morally responsible choice in which it is determined that compliance and truthfulness needs to be sacrificed to the higher good of mission and troop support. Here there is an acknowledgement that one is in some sense lying but also that it is being done in the service of fairness, keeping one's promise to honor a higher duty, or even the sanctity of life. This kind of reasoning believes that there is a genuine conflict between relative goods and choosing the higher value is the burden of ethical leadership in an imperfect world especially as that is experienced in combat. This perspective resembles Sissela Bok's "third excuse" for lying. This type of excuse "offers moral reasons to show that a lie ought to, under the circumstances, be allowed. People look for moral reasons when they are troubled or caught short; and generally when they need to persuade themselves or others that the usual presumption against lying is outweighed in their particular case."

27. Ibid., 17–18.
28. Ibid., 20.
29. Ibid., 22.

Their reasons then range from the prevention of harm to the promotion of the good.[30]

We are all aware that this sort of rationale that Bok describes operates on an individual basis in everyday life, sometimes involving the inescapable choice of choosing the lesser of evils. Certainly lying on behalf of the greater good and the avoidance of harm is a justification invoked in the political sphere, in matters of diplomacy and national security, and in wartime. As Winston Churchill famously put the case, "In wartime . . . truth is so precious that she should always be attended by a bodyguard of lies."[31] Depending on one's point of view Churchill's comment could be considered a remark worthy of Machiavelli or an elegantly stated realistic appraisal of how things are under the tragic conditions of war. However, the excuse that a realistic view of conflictual circumstances justifies the sacrifice of truth can be an enticing invitation to self-deception and self-justification. Of course, one may also argue that many choices to forego the truth in the interest of what is claimed to be a higher good or lesser evil may not be the product of an agonized moral struggle. It may be a somewhat Machiavellian calculus that the end justifies the means and no excuse is required.

From a Christian ethics perspective, James Wall, reflecting on lying in public life, offers this stinging assessment:

> Lying sometimes may help us accomplish and immediate goal. . . .
> But each lie undermines the network of trust on which relationships rely. Lying is wrong, furthermore, because it violates our covenant with God, a covenant which sustains us in our human frailty. Without a moral principle backing our daily intercourse, we are left to function with the utilitarian assumptions that if it works, do it; if it feels good try it. The bottom line, maximum return and cost efficiency become the trinity for those who assume there is no general moral principle by which we are meant to live.[32]

The Army study does not approach the problem from Wall's faith-based standpoint but it shares with him the concern that lying, even if considered a trivial case, serves to undermine the trust on which relationships depend. "Tolerating a level of dishonesty in areas deemed trivial or unimportant results in the degradation of trust that is vital to the military profession."[33]

30. Bok, *Lying*, 75–76.

31. Quoted in Thielicke, *Theological Ethics*, 541.

32. Wall, "Politics and the Darkness of Lying."

33. Wong and Gerras, *Lying to Ourselves*, 25. The report quotes Bok in support of this

And this is the key concern for the report. Regardless of whether the deceit is considered trivial, represents a genuine ethical struggle, or is a way to protect oneself from censure or the appearance of flawed leadership, a culture in which dishonesty is allowed or even expected is not healthy. Thus, the report, *in the interest of telling the truth,* says that the Army must first acknowledge the problem on the way to changing the culture.

In the end, all rationalizations aside, even those that seem understandable if not justifiable, for the report it comes down to honest leadership. Recall Nancy Sherman's account of the level of honesty that characterized the post-mission debriefings of that Navy squadron, even to the point of senior officers being ready to admit mistakes. The researchers conclude that something different is often the case.

> While junior officers freely describe their struggles in maintaining their integrity in a culture that breeds dishonesty, senior officers are often reluctant to admit their personal failings in front of subordinates (or in the case of very senior officers their peers). . . . They can easily lecture about the ideals of integrity and honor, but find it extremely difficult to admit that they too have encountered (and currently live with) a culture that condones dishonesty.[34]

What is called for is to lead truthfully. Leading truthfully means that senior officers need to take on the task of restraint in the reducing the overwhelming number of requirement placed on junior officers, a burden that compromises their integrity. Prioritizing among the many requests that come down for this or that data will require the courage of honest appraisal in engaging those who are initiating those demands. "Leading truthfully dismantles the façade of mutually agreed deception by putting considerations of the integrity of the profession back into the decision making process."[35]

In chapter 6 we dealt with the closely interwoven values or virtues of honor and integrity. We saw there these values or virtues are emphasized in all the services. The study of lying in the Army echoes the central concern for integrity in matters of truthfulness. It also recognizes the necessity for the organizational culture to deal with the circumstances that foster dishonesty and discourage truthfulness.

Of course, truth-telling is a problem in all walks of life. For myriad reasons people find lying expedient when under pressure or in fear of

---

threat, *Lying,* 21.

34. Wong and Gerras, *Lying to Ourselves,* 29.

35. Ibid., 32.

exposure and the consequences that might follow. The rationalizations are probably as numerous as the types of lies we tell. And excuses are often plausible in an imperfect world that frequently presents us with bad choices. Chaplains have a pastoral duty to appreciate the strain on conscience that many may be feeling. Depending on the access they may have to the channels of decision, empathy for those struggling with bad choices should lead to advocacy for change as an aspect of support for honesty. The report's critique recognizes what neighbor love also understands, namely, how important honesty is for the trust essential to a cohesive community. Truth-telling as a principle of *agape* is, like that love itself, relational, geared to the well-being of the other and ready to risk the consequences of honesty to that end.

Transition: The Importance of Maintaining Trust

Trust is an abiding characteristic of all life together. We cannot avoid interactions that require a certain amount of trust in the other party whether that is our physician, our teachers, our financial advisor, government agencies established to protect us, our parents, our spouse, etc. In these and other relationships of trust we entrust ourselves, surrender something of our life to the other party. Entrusting ourselves to the other as an expression of our trust in that person or entity and the acceptance of our trust by the trusted party entails a commitment to honor that trust with active concern for our well-being. It is a commitment, spoken or unspoken, to honor our trust, to be trustworthy and to not violate that trust. Nowhere is the relationship of trusting, entrusting, and being trustworthy more essential than in the life of the military. When one joins the military one is committed to follow orders and be obedient to those in command. This pledge is a promise. It means that you are placing your very life in the hands of your leaders; it is a monumental act of trust. But the matter is not one-sided. There is a corollary obligation on the part of those in command that they are worthy of that trust. Furthermore, trustworthiness becomes an expectation of all who are serving together. As we have stated earlier, warriors need to trust each other; their lives depend upon it. Mutual trust in one another is integral to the culture of military service at all levels of interaction.

The values or virtues of the services discussed in chapters 4, 5, and 6 are essential to the building and maintenance of trust. We have sought to correlate these values with the principles which embody love's commitment to the neighbor: respect for autonomy, sanctity of life, justice, truth-telling, and promise-keeping. Each of these in their own way express in motive and action the commitment one has to the dignity, worth, and well-being of the other that is the foundation of trust.

It is certainly true that violations of trust in the civilian world can cause lasting damage to individuals and groups. One thinks of the trust Native Americans placed in government treaties that were subsequently broken by the government. Violations of trust by corporations like Enron or the financial scam of a Bernie Madoff had dire consequences for those affected. The greed that perpetrated the mortgage loan disaster sent the economy into a tailspin and contributed to the rise in unemployment. Breaches of trust through acts of infidelity have broken up marriage and family, leaving lasting scars on the lives of spouses and children. If one has lived long enough or is observant enough one has come to understand, sometimes first hand, the sorry results of a violated trust. It is endemic to a sinful world.

In military life a breach of trust can be fatal, as we have said. Violation of trust, a sense of betrayal by those in command or by civilian authorities, may also be implicated in cases of moral injury as earlier discussed. We recall the statement of retired Army General James M. Dubik that putting one's life on the line fighting in a war that is unjust, imprudent, or unnecessary can give rise to a sense of betrayal on the part of those who sent you into battle. This treats the warrior like an object to be manipulated and not a person to be valued, which the general suggests could be the ultimate moral injury.[36]

In the close knit and highly structured, interdependent life of those in the military a violation of trust affecting the individual, though not fatal, can have serious deleterious effects beyond the pain suffered by the victim. For example, one may tend to think that instances of sexual abuse are largely a matter of individual suffering on the part of the victim. However, the consequences are more far-reaching than even the personal experience of violation of one's person, one's dignity, betrayal of trust, and shame and moral injury. While sexual abuse is first and foremost a matter of concern for the well-being of the person affected, to the extent that such instances of abuse are widespread they can undermine the sense of mutual trust and commitment to one another. Respect for one another in matters of sexuality is an essential component in the building of social trust. The loss of this

36. See above, 112.

social trust threatens the "unit cohesion" so essential to mission readiness and mission accomplishment, which then has its own further consequences.

Chapter Eleven

Safe and Sacred Spaces

PREVIOUSLY WE HAVE EMPHASIZED that the concerns of the Christian ethic in relation to military life include the moral responsibility the citizenry in general and faith communities in particular have for the support of those who we send to war. Specifically, we said

> In terms of the just war tradition, which has been observed inside and outside the churches, the principle that a war to be just must be declared by a legitimate authority, means for a democratic society that the citizenry take ownership for that declaration and responsibility for its casualties, whether physical or spiritual, including all who share in the losses of war. The Christian church along with other faiths have a vocational obligation to lead the way in their own witness of caring.[1]

There are various ways in which such ownership can find expression in support of our service men and women; the needs are many. We have chosen to focus on the morally injured and their need for healing. We have done so because of its connection to the deep spiritual and emotional dimension of the ethical focus of the book. Yet even as we highlight the involvement of both chaplains and church in the healing of the moral wounds of war, we need to recognize that our faith communities, which are part of our civilian society, share in the reality of a divide that exists between the military and civilian life. This divide hampers a better level of civilian understanding, concern, and involvement in the needs of those in military service.

1. See above, 102.

The Civilian-Military Divide

What are the sources of this divide? To begin with, according to a National Public Radio report, military personnel (active duty, National Guard, Air National Guard, and reserves) make up less than 1 percent of the US population.[2] Clearly, then, very few American families are directly affected or personally involved in military concerns by having one of their own engaged in war or some other facet of military service. A similar observation could be made about some of our national leaders. An August 13, 2015 article in the *Los Angeles Times* makes the salient point that the recent wars were authorized by a US Congress that has the lowest rate of military service in history and were led by three successive presidents who have never served on active duty. The *Times* article goes on to note that of the small percentage of the population in military service, 80 percent come from families in which a parent or sibling was also in the military. There is virtually a separate warrior class, isolated in many respects from the general population. When not deployed they live apart from the civilian world on bases that are basically "gated communities." But that privilege and distance is part of a problem for both the military and the civilian population. As one World War II veteran interviewee observed, "Today's soldiers carry a heavier burden because the public has been disconnected from the universal responsibility and personal commitment required to fight and win wars."[3]

James Fallows's article, "The Tragedy of the American Military," published in *The Atlantic,* is perhaps even more pointed in analyzing the civilian-military divide. Despite overblown praise for the military, Fallows observes, "I am not aware of any midterm race for House or Senate in which matters of war and peace—as opposed to immigration, Obamacare, voting rights, tax rates, the Ebola scare—were first-tier campaign issues on either side. . . . This reverent but disengaged attitude toward the military—we love the troops, but we'd rather not think about them—has become so familiar that we assume it is the American norm."[4] Fallows observes further that ours is a country "willing to do anything for its military but take it seriously." As a consequence, the military pays a price for the lack of public scrutiny in the unexamined willingness to send troops on unending, unwinnable

2. National Public Radio, "By the Numbers: Today's Military."
3. Zucchino and Cloud, "U.S. Military and Civilians Are Increasingly Divided."
4. Fallows, "The Tragedy of the American Military."

missions, despite their being the finest fighting force in the world. Fallows tells the story of a marine officer who did four tours of duty in Iraq. The officer, named Seth Moulton, spoke of how disconnected America is from the small group of warriors doing the country's work. He did not believe that the country cared how the troops were doing. In a telling anecdote Moulton related the comment of a young marine in his platoon, "Sir, you should run for Congress someday. So this shit doesn't happen again."[5]

Theologian Ted Peters, suggests provocatively that the American soldier is the nation's "invisible scapegoat." It is not the soldier him- or herself that is visibly, personally, the scapegoat; they are truly heroes. It is rather the scapegoat mechanism whereby the nation sanctifies and justifies itself and its messianic mission by the sacrifice of its wounded and dead warriors. But, Peters continues, "Under fire in the war zone, some of our scapegoated soldiers have suffered acutely not only from physical injury but also from misunderstanding, confusion, betrayal, and guilt. In certain cases their moral universe has collapsed." This is the moral injury of the broken soul.[6]

Nancy Sherman reports that returning veterans often shut out civilians, including family members, as unworthy of receiving their trust. If one has not served in the military, one does not know what war is like. Resentment often expressed at the civilian's "Thank you for your service" fits in here. This resentment gives too many civilians the permission to withdraw from helping for fear of being meddlesome. She says this myth needs to be "debunked by both sides."[7] But can it be?

Bridging the Divide: Safe and Sacred Spaces

A key to bridging the gap between the two worlds, civilian and military, may well be the trust many wounded warriors have shown in both chaplains and civilian clergy, and in the faith-based organizations they encounter as they return to society.

1.6 million Americans have served in Iraq or Afghanistan since the beginning of the global war on terror. It is reported that nearly 790,000 veterans have been released from the military services and have returned to our communities with more yet to come as the military draws down to near historic lows. In April 2008, the Rand Corporation released the results of a

5. Ibid.
6. Peters, *Sin Boldly*, 237–50.
7. Sherman, *Afterwar*, 119–20.

study that found that nearly 20 percent, or one in five, returning veterans reported symptoms of post-traumatic stress disorder or major depression. Significantly, only about half of these veterans sought treatment for their condition, and yet the Department of Veterans Affairs has treated more than 68,000 veterans for post-traumatic stress disorder. What of those who did not seek mental health professionals for help? It is well documented that military service members and their families continually find it difficult to seek the help of mental health providers for PTSD, marital and family issues, and other needs. They do, however, turn with surprising frequency to chaplains, pastoral counselors, and other clergypersons for help. "Spiritual care providers, such as chaplains, pastoral counselors, and clergypersons are a key part of the US mental health care system, and they serve particularly unique roles in caring for many veterans and service members with mental health needs. Particularly in the military where fears persist about mental health treatment potentially leading to negative career repercussions or perceptions that one is weak, chaplains are often considered a safer, trusted, and more confidential option."[8]

A 2015 Rand Corporation report echoes the findings that chaplains are trusted as safe because of concerns for privacy and confidentiality.[9] Military chaplains conduct their pastoral counseling under official policy. The following is the policy on confidential communication under Secretary of the Navy Instruction (SECNAV INSTRUCTION 1730.9.). It reads in part:

> This instruction provides policy on confidential communications to Navy chaplains. The unconstrained ability to discuss personal matters in complete privacy encourages full and complete disclosure by personnel and family members seeking chaplain assistance. Such disclosure establishes a sacred trust, facilitates increased morale and mission readiness, and benefits both the individual and the institution.

The other services operate with similar policies.

The 2015 report extends this pattern of trust to civilian clergy and faith-based organizations" (FBOs), which include religious congregations and coordinating bodies, as well as faith-based nongovernmental organizations. Indeed, the report allowed that experience with chaplains while in service influenced veterans to regard faith-based organizations as safe places. *We need to emphasize at this juncture that it is imperative that*

---

8. Rand Corporation, "One in Five Iraq and Afghanistan Veterans Suffer."
9. Werber et. al., "Faith Based Organizations and Veteran Reintegration," 8.

military chaplains and leaders of faith-based communities seek each other out to maximize the benefits of their shared trust. The importance of FBOs as partners in mental health and social services is part of a current trend. And FBOs, especially congregations, are particularly well-suited to the needs of veterans because they are all over the map and embedded in the local communities to which veterans return. They may have a better understanding of veterans' individual needs. Given the trust that clergy or other members for the faith community may enjoy, veterans may be more willing to disclose their needs. "Further, additional research suggests that local clergy tend to have a global and holistic view of veteran's needs, while health care providers (physicians, psychologists, social workers, and nurses) tend to focus more on the specific issues that assist in making a differential clinical diagnosis."[10] This latter point correlates well with our earlier discussion of Warren Kinghorn's concern with the limits of the medical model in the treatment of moral injury and his advocacy for the addition of a spiritual approach.[11]

The Rand study of 2015 asked "What support do FBOs provide veterans?" One interviewee from a faith community spoke in terms of war as a spiritual issue. For many veterans clinical approaches are not experienced as fully effective in dealing with the spiritual character of moral injury. Accordingly, spiritual care through various spiritual activities such as healing retreats and pastoral care are important. Faith-based communities are recognizing that problems of veteran reintegration caused by the feelings of isolation and alienation that inhere in the wounded soul of the morally injured. Support for the morally wounded, interviewees of the faith communities stressed, "must come from a 'benevolent moral authority' in an atmosphere free from judgment, with unconditional acceptance."[12] These characteristics of care are one of the ways safe and sacred space can be created.[13]

Of course, by the very nature of their calling clergy are trained and equipped to address the salient spiritual dynamics related to moral injury.

10. Ibid., 3–8

11. See above, 100.

12. Werber et.al., "Faith Based Organizations and Veteran Reintegration," 4–6.

13. Though not specifically related to the needs of veterans, a number of studies have shown the value of clergy in engaging issue of mental health and of the preference often shown for their help and support. See, for example, Wang, Berglund, and Kessler, "Patterns and Correlates of Contacting Clergy for Mental Disorders in the United States"; and Hall and Gjestfjeld, "Clergy: A Partner in Rural Mental Health."

This vocational formation, together with the aforementioned importance of their pledge of confidentially make chaplains and other clergy critical to the establishment of safe and sacred space. Jonathan Shay, clinical psychologist Brett Litz of Boston University, and others have come to believe that warriors suffering from these types of moral wounds must have a safe and sacred place in which they can be aided in asking themselves hard questions designed to identify the nature of the moral wound they have experienced. This includes questions such as, "What currently is most distressing and most haunting for you?" These and other questions are aimed at helping the morally wounded warrior identify the three most common feeling associated with moral wounds: guilt, shame, and alienation.[14]

It might be said that moral wounds are caused by the move from *cosmos* into *chaos*, which is the nature of war itself. Cosmos, chaos, or some combination of both seems to be for us the only choices regarding the type of world in which we can live. We need order in our lives and in the world surrounding us so we strive to live out our being in an ordered world in which there are certain shared values. Mircea Eliade said, "The experience of sacred space makes possible the founding of the world. The manifestation of the sacred ontologically founds the world."[15] Eliade is here arguing for the notion that sacred space is a place where one experiences life in cosmos versus chaos.

Honor, courage, fidelity, etc. are values that have been embraced by warriors in an attempt to bring cosmos into the experience of the chaos of war. These values are intended to bring some sense of order to the chaos of combat and thus preserve the humanity of friend and foe alike in the inhuman and soul-debasing experience of war. This striving for cosmos is for the Christian warrior a quest to sustain a commitment to *agape*, love for the neighbor, even under the duress of war. We have attempted in earlier chapters to show the possibility of correlating the the core values of the military services with the ethics of neighbor love. The just war tradition, with its roots in such Christian leaders as Augustine and Aquinas, has served as a limiting force in the conduct of war for centuries. The Rules of Engagement adopted by the military of the United States and other countries are a modern attempt at limiting the dimensions of chaos in war and thereby mitigating the damage to the humanity of warriors caused by armed conflict. In our broken world where war remains a tragic reality, the Christian ethic of

---

14. Bebinger, Freemark, and Guntzel, "'Moral Injury.'"

15. Eliade, *The Sacred and the Profane*, 12.

love seeks to create cosmos in the midst of threatening chaos. Jesus' love commandment is grounded in his promise that he has come that all may have life and have it abundantly (John 10:10). It is this Gospel promise of abundant and endless life that transforms all things with the energy of hope and sanctifies our world of God's creation. For wounded warriors, then, sacred space is not a place of our own creation but exists wherever God reveals God's self in the gathering of two or more. American Legion and Veterans of Foreign Wars (VFW) posts, churches and pubs, coffee shops and athletic fields, work places and foxholes, high places and low, in the presence of angels or demons, in places sacred and places profane, God finds us where we are as our ally.

In Romans 8:35–39 St. Paul writes,

> Who will separate us from the love of Christ? Will hardship, or distress, or persecution, or famine, or nakedness, or peril, or sword? As it is written, "For your sake we are being killed all day long; we are accounted as sheep to be slaughtered." No, in all these things we are more than conquerors through him who loved us. For I am convinced that neither death, nor life, nor angels, nor rulers, nor things present, nor things to come, nor powers, nor height, nor depth, nor anything else in all creation, will be able to separate us from the love of God in Christ Jesus our Lord.

This well-known and well-loved text could well serve as the text for this entire book. If we are talking about the tough and even terrible choices one must make in the throes of combat, this promise is there for faith and the courage to go forward. If we are talking of the spiritual struggles of the chaplain to live up to the seemingly impossible spiritual standard and challenges of their vocation, that promise is there for faith and the courage to go forward. If we are talking about Christians in positions of command who struggle with the ethical intricacies of drone warfare, the limits of prisoner interrogation, and maintaining the integrity of stated values, this promise is there to say, "you are not alone," and God's acceptance is with you all the way as you navigate the imperfections of a broken world. If you are a wounded soul, living the nightmare of shame, self-doubt, and loss of meaning and hope, as a Christian community we have the moral obligation to bring you this promise that you may go forward and live.

Bibliography

Allen, Joseph. *Love and Conflict*. Nashville: Abingdon, 1984.

Bebinger, Martha, Samara Freemark, and Jeff Severns Guntzel. "Moral Injury: When Soldiers Betray Their Sense of Right and Wrong." WBUR Boston. www.wbur.org/2013/06/21/moral-injury-illustration.

Binau, Brad A. "Shame and the Human Predicament." In *Counseling and the Human Predicament: A Study of Sin Guilt and Forgiveness*, edited by L. Alden and D. Renner, 127–43. Grand Rapids: Baker, 1989.

Bell, Daniel M., Jr. "Let Character Prevail." *Christianity Today*, August 1, 2011, 65.

Bok, Sissela. *Lying: Moral Choice in Public and Private Life*. New York: Pantheon, 1978.

Bonhoeffer, Dietrich. *Discipleship*. Dietrich Bonhoeffer Works 4. Edited by Geffrey B. Kelly and John D. Godsey. Translated by Barbara Green and Reinhard Krauss. Minneapolis: Fortress, 2003.

———. *Ethics*. Dietrich Bonhoeffer Works 6. Edited by Clifford J. Green. Translated by Reinhard Krauss, Charles C. West, and Douglas Stott. Minneapolis: Fortress, 2005.

Boyatzis, R. E. *The Competent Manager: A Model for Effective Leadership*. Hoboken, NJ: John Wiley and Sons, 1982.

Bradley, Peter. "Is Battlefield Mercy Killing Morally Justifiable?" *Canadian Military Journal* 11 (November 1, 2010) 7–14.

Bright, John. *The Kingdom of God*. New York: Abingdon, 1953.

Brock, Rita Nakashima, and Gabriella Lettini. *Soul Repair: Recovering from Moral Injury after War*. Boston: Beacon, 2012.

Childs, James M., Jr. *Ethics in the Community of Promise: Faith, Formation, and Decision*. Minneapolis: Fortress, 2006.

Coll, Steve. "Remote Control." *The New Yorker*, May 6, 2013, 78–79.

Cook, Martin L. *The Moral Warrior: Ethics and Service in the U.S. Military*. Albany, NY: State University of New York Press, 2004.

Department of Defense Law of War Manual. Washington, DC: Office of the General Council Department of Defense, 2015.

De Pree, Max. *Leadership is an Art*. New York: Dell, 1989.

Eberle, Christopher J. "God, War, and Conscience." *Journal of Religious Ethics* 35:3 (2007) 479–507.

Eliade, Mircea. *The Sacred and the Profane: The Nature of Religion*. Orlando: Harcourt, 1957.

Engel, Richard. "Former Drone Operator Says He's Haunted by His Part in More than 1,600 Deaths." http://investigations.nbcnews.com/_news/2013/06/06/18787450-former-drone-operator-says-hes-haunted-by-his-part.

Evangelical Lutheran Church in America. "For Peace in God's World." August 20, 1995.

Facione, Peter A. "Critical Thinking: What It Is and Why It Counts." http://www.insightassessment.com/content/dowload/1176/7580/fild/what&why.pdf.

Fallows, James. "The Tragedy of the American Military." The Atlantic (January/February 2015). http://theatlantic.com/magazine/archive/2015/01/the-tragedy-of-the-american-military/385316.

Formula of Concord, Article VIII, 44. The Book of Concord. Edited by Robert Kolb and Timothy J. Wengert. Minneapolis: Fortress, 2000.

French, Peter A. War and Moral Dissonance. Cambridge: Cambridge University Press, 2011.

Gaudium et Spes. Documents of Vatican II. December 7, 1965.

Hall, Douglas John. The Cross in Our Context: Jesus and the Suffering World. Minneapolis: Fortress, 2003.

Hall, S. Allana, and Christopher D. Gjestfjeld. "Clergy: A Partner in Rural Mental Health." Journal of Rural Mental Health 37:1 (2013) 50–57.

Han, Sang-Ehil, Paul Lewis Metzger, and Terry C. Muck. "Christian Hospitality and Pastoral Practices from an Evangelical Perspective." Theological Education 47:1 (2012) 11–13.

Hoekema, David A. "A Practical Christian Pacifism." Christian Century, October 22, 1986, 917–19.

Holt, Steve. "Hellfire from Above." Sojourners, July 2013, 22.

Janis, I. L. "Groupthink." Psychology Today 5:6 (November 1971) 43–46, 74–76.

Jelinek, Pauline. "Some Casualties are 'Wounded Souls.'" The Columbus Dispatch, February 24, 2013.

Keizer, Herman, Jr. "Stop drone strikes and the moral injury of their pilots." http://www.star-telegram.com/opinion/opn-columns-blogs/othervoices/article 9702050.html.

Kime, Patricia. "Incidents of Rape in Military Much Higher than Previously Reported." http://www.militarytimes.com/story/military/pentagon/2014/12/04/pentagon-rand-sexual-assault-reports/19883155/.

Kinghorn, Warren. "Combat Trauma and Moral Fragmentation: A Theological Account of Moral Injury." Journal of Christian Ethics 32:2 (2012) 57–74.

Küng, Hans. Global Responsibility: In Search of a New World Ethic. New York: Crossroad, 1991.

Lasson, Kenneth. "Religious Liberty in the Military: The First Amendment under 'Friendly Fire.'" Journal of Law and Religion 9:2 (1992) 471–99, 493.

Lauritzen, Paul. The Ethics of Interrogation: Professional Responsibility in an Age of Terror. Washington, DC: Georgetown University Press, 2013.

———. "'Lawful but Awful': The Moral Perils of Drone Warfare." Commonweal, January 23, 2015, 16–18.

Leslie, Kristen J. "Pastoral Care in a New Public: Lessons Learned in the Public Square." Journal of Pastoral Theology 18:2 (Winter 2008) 80–99.

Lovin, Robin W. Christian Ethics: An Essential Guide. Nashville: Abingdon, 2000.

Luther, Martin, "Heidelberg Disputation." In Luther's Works, vol. 31, translated by Harold Grimm, 37–69. Philadelphia: Muhlenberg, 1957.

———. "Temporal Authority: To What Extent It Should Be Obeyed." In *Luther's Works*, vol. 45, 12–126. American ed. Philadelphia: Muhlenberg, 1962.

Maguire, Daniel C. *A Moral Creed for All Christians*. Minneapolis: Fortress, 2005.

Marlantes, Karl. *What It Is Like to Go to War*. New York: Atlantic Monthly, 2011.

Marine Corps Times. "Commandant: Who We Are and Who We Are Not." Video interview with General Amos and Sergeant Major Barrett. http://archive.marinecorpstimes. com/VideoNetwork//2394437955001/Commandant-Who-We-Are-and-Who-We-Are-Not.

Mason, R. Chuck, and Cynthia Brougher. *Military Personnel and Freedom of Religious Expression: Selected Legal Issues*. Washington, DC: Congressional Research Service, 2010.

Mastroianni, George R. "The Person-Situation Debate: Implications for Military Leadership and Civilian-Military Relations." *Journal of Military Ethics* 10:1 (2011) 9–10.

Moltmann, Jürgen. *In the End—The Beginning: The Life of Hope*. Translated by Margaret Kohl. Minneapolis: Fortress, 2004.

———. *The Trinity and the Kingdom: The Doctrine of God*. New York: Harper and Row, 1981.

Morris, Vic. "Fostering Spiritual Resiliency in Warriors." *Dialogue*, Spring 2013, 10–12.

Mount, Eric, Jr. "Terrorism, Torture, and Conscience." *Theology Today* 65 (2008) 356–67.

Nash, William P., Teresa L. Marino Carper, Mary Alice Mills, Teresa Au, Abigail Goldsmith, and Brett T. Litz. "Psychometric Evaluation of Moral Injury Events Scale." *Military Medicine* 178:6 (2013) 646–52.

National Center for PTSD. "PTSD." www.ptsd.va.gov.

National Public Radio. "By the Numbers: Today's Military." July 3, 2011.

Niebuhr, H. Richard. *Christ and Culture*. New York: Harper & Row, 1951.

Niebuhr, Reinhold. "Justice and Love." In *Love and Justice: Selections from the Shorter Writings of Reinhold Niebuhr*, edited by D. B. Robertson, 27–29. Philadelphia: Westminster, 1957.

Pannenberg, Wolfhart. *Jesus—God and Man*. Translated by Lewis Wilkins and Duane A. Priebe. Philadelphia: Westminster, 1968.

Paul, Richard, and Linda Elder. *The Miniature Guide to Critical Thinking Concepts and Tools*. Tomales, CA: Foundation for Critical Thinking, 2008.

Peters, Ted. *God—The World's Future: Systematic Theology for a New Era*. 2nd ed. Minneapolis: Fortress, 2000.

———. *Sin Boldly: Justifying Faith for Fragile and Broken Souls*. Minneapolis: Fortress, 2015.

Rand Corporation. "One in Five Iraq and Afghanistan Veterans Suffer from PTSD or Major Depression." April 17, 2008. http://rand.org/news/press/2008/04/17.html.

Recommendations and Report of the Task Force on US Drone Policy. Washington, DC: Stimson Center, 2014.

Rice, Jim. "War Crimes and Misdemeanors." *Sojourners*, August 2012, 23.

Robinson, Paul. "Introduction: Ethics Education in the Military." In *Ethics Education in the Military*, edited by Paul Robinson, Nigel De Lee, and Don Carrick, 1–12. Farnham, UK: Ashgate, 2008.

Schuette, Rob. "Spiritual Resiliency Helps Soldiers Weather Life's Traumas." www.army. mil.

Shay, Johnathan. "Casualties." *Daedalus* 140:3 (2011) 179–88.

Sherman, Nancy. *Afterwar: Healing the Moral Wounds of Our Soldiers.* New York: Oxford University Press, 2015.

———. *The Untold War: Inside the Hearts, Minds, and Souls of Our Soldiers.* New York: W. W. Norton, 2010.

Skerker, Michael. *An Ethics of Interrogation.* Chicago: University of Chicago Press, 2010.

"Spiritual Resiliency Helps Soldiers Weather Life's Traumas." http://www.army.mil/article/31653/spiritual-resiliency-helps-soldiers-weather-trauma.

Stone, Rupert. "Beyond Torture: The Science of Interrogating Terrorists." *Newsweek*, June 9, 2015. http://www.newsweek.com/2015/06/19/beyond-torture-new-science-interrogating terrorists-340944.html.

Thielicke, Helmut. *Theological Ethics,* vol. 1. Edited by William H. Lazareth. Philadelphia: Fortress, 1966.

Tillich, Paul. *Systematic Theology,* vol. 3. Chicago: University of Chicago Press, 1963.

Thrall, James H. "Being a Peace Church in a World of War." http://archive.episcopalchurch.org/dcdaily_17597_ENG_HTM.htm.

Thomas, George F. *Christian Ethics and Moral Philosophy.* New York: Charles Scribner's Sons, 1955.

United States Conference of Catholic Bishops. "Declaration on Conscientious Objection and Selective Conscientious Objection." October 21, 1971.

Wall, James M. "Politics and the Darkness of Lying." *Christian Century*, November 6, 1991, 1019.

Wang, Philip S., Patricia A. Berglund, and Ronald C. Kessler. "Patterns and Correlates of Contacting Clergy for Mental Disorders in the United States." *Health Studies Research* 38:2 (April 2003) 647–73.

Watson, Julie. "Military Drone Operators Can Feel Emotional Strains of War." *Huffington Post.* http://www.huffingtonpost.com.

———. "Souls in Anguish Tortured by War Memories." *Pittsburgh Tribune-Review,* August 16, 2015.

"War." In the *Stanford Encyclopedia of Philosophy.* http://plat.stanfor.edu/entries/war.

Werber, Laura, Kathryn Pitkin, Mollie Rudnick, Margaret C. Harrell, and Diana Naranjo. "Faith Based Organizations and Veteran Reintegration." Rand Corporation (2015).

Wester, Franklin Eric. "'Soldier Spirituality' in a Combat Zone and Preliminary Findings about Correlations with Ethics and Resilience." Unpublished report.

Wigglesworth, Cindy. "Spiritual Intelligence and Why It Matters." Deep Change. www.deepchange.com.

The Witness of U.S. Lutherans on Peace, War, and Conscience: A Social Document from the Lutheran Council in the U.S.A., 1973. http://download.elca.org/ELCA%20Resource%20Repository/Peace_War_Conscience.CU.pdf?_ga=1.254689928.186299913.

Wong, Leonard, and Stephen J. Gerras. *Lying to Ourselves: Dishonesty in the Army Profession.* Carlisle, PA: Strategic Studies Institute and United States Army War College Press, 2015.

Wright, N. T. *The Challenge of Jesus: Rediscovering who Jesus Was and Is.* Downers Grove, IL: InterVarsity, 1999.

Zucchino, David, and David S. Cloud. "U.S. Military and Civilians Are Increasingly Divided." *Los Angeles Times,* August 13, 2015.

Made in the USA
Monee, IL
04 February 2022

90595262R00094